'02

Merry Christmas
Connie,

I know you don't
care for Victoriana
but this "Blue" "Book"
just said "You" to me.
Much Love and
Big Hugs!
Barb + Joe

BLUE&WHITE
in your home

BLUE &

WHITE
in your home

Lisa Skolnik and the Editors of
Victoria Magazine

HEARST BOOKS

NEW YORK

A Roundtable Press Book

Library of Congress Cataloging-in-Publication Data

Skolnik, Lisa
    Blue and white in your home / by Lisa Skolnik and the Editors of Victoria
      p. cm
    At head of title: Victoria
    ISBN 1-58816-055-6
     1. Blue in interior decoration. 2. White in interior decoration. I. Victoria
(New York, N.Y.) II. Title

NK2115.5.C6 S59 2001
747'.94—dc21

                                                  2001024778

For Victoria:
Peggy Kennedy, Editor-in-Chief
Nora Negron, Art Director

For Roundtable Press, Inc.
DIRECTORS: Susan E. Meyer, Marsha Melnick, Julie Merberg
DESIGN: Joel Avirom
SENIOR EDITOR: Carol Spier
EDITORIAL ASSISTANT: Sara Newberry

Printed in the USA

First Edition

1 2 3 4 5 6 7 8 9 10

foreword

If I were asked to recommend one color scheme practically guaranteed to work in any room, it would most certainly be blue and white. I know I am not alone in my appreciation of this timeless pairing. When people are asked their favorite color combination, many, if not most, will respond, blue and white. Whether the hues are brightly crisp and clean or whisper-soft, a room dressed in blue and white never fails to refresh and soothe.

Gathering the pieces for a blue and white room can resemble a United Nations conference. It's a combination that transcends borders and speaks any language. Think of tiles from Portugal or Morocco, Delft from Holland, Spanish or Italian pottery, English china, French toile, Chinese porcelain, and Japanese ikat fabrics. Happily, the many shades of blue seem to marry well with each other. The more hues you mix, the more foolproof the blend. When does the sea clash with the sky? In one kitchen, a designer I admire, who was obsessed with blue and white, packed a hutch with every imaginable hue of blue: a mismatched jumble of patterned porcelain, pottery and enamelware, even, tucked away on the top shelf, the proverbial sink. The unique display produced pure visual delight.

At Victoria, one of our missions is to inspire people to surround themselves with style, comfort, and beauty. In this book, we decided to examine the ways blue and white can be used to achieve this goal. The palette works so well with so many periods and styles, whether formal or casual, traditional or a personal mix, that we were delighted to find an almost endless array of possibilities, to see how many ways others had found to bring blue and white into their homes. With all the beautiful rooms assembled here, I am sure that each time you turn the page, you will find yourself newly inspired.

PEGGY KENNEDY
EDITOR-IN-CHIEF
VICTORIA MAGAZINE

5

contents

introduction

Since ancient times people have drawn inspiration for the decoration of their homes, domestic wares, and clothing from nature. When you consider that we see white clouds billowing in azure skies by day and platinum stars punctuating inky heavens at night, it is no wonder that blue and white are so frequently combined by designers. Indeed, the blue and white color scheme has been adapted by cultures throughout history—in sometimes vivid and other times subtle but always lovely hues. It figured prominently in the mosaic murals of ancient Byzantium, Greece, and Rome; was immortalized on porcelain and china in the East and the West; and has graced the exteriors and interiors of regal and humble abodes for centuries.

9

Travel the world today, and you will likely find blue and white adorning the exterior of a seaside villa in Italy or Greece, a fancifully trimmed cottage in Scandinavia, a tidy clapboard home in New England, a frothy painted lady in the deep South, or a bungalow in California. Even commercial structures, whether encrusted in white marble or clad in reflective glass, mirror the image of the sky and clouds around them. And this palette remains as popular for our interiors and domestic trappings as when blue and white dyes and pigments were first discovered.

A seventeenth-century country house in Europe or the New World might have sported walls, doors, shutters, and wood furnishings painted soft shades of blue; upholstery swathed in subdued blue textiles; and shelves lined with blue and white Chinese export pottery. By the eighteenth century

An interpretation of blue and white that will appeal to every preference is exemplified by this cool, elegant table setting with shades of silvery blue and icy white. The combination is a perennially popular choice for the table, and is so versatile that any effect can be achieved with the right accessories. Here a gossamer blue liner paired with pure white linens is all it takes to set the tone and bring out the other touches of blue in the setting.

distinctive shades of blue with cloudy or ashy overtones, such as soldier, slate, calico, Dutch and French blue, were popular; today we associate these with the colonial era in America and the Georgian period in England. By the beginning of the nineteenth century, brilliant lapis, royal, Prussian, Persian, marine, and berry blues were being paired with lustrous and bright whites in Regency and Federal homes. Later the Shakers chose clear, deep blues, sometimes with soft gray overtones, to contrast with clean white; Victorians embraced blues both rich and dark or soft and powdery; and designers of the Arts and Crafts movement glorified the blues found naturally in flowers and herbs. The romance with blue and white continued throughout the twentieth century, with the steely blues and icy whites of the Art Deco period, the primary or eye-popping blues and whites of Modernism, and the revivalist hues of every ilk conjured up before the new millennium.

But blue and white is hardly a Western invention. The color blue was first used in the Near East and is thought to have first emerged as a decorative hue around 4500 B.C. in Mesopotamia. Other ancient cultures all over the world also embraced the hue, as evidenced by the fact that the Peruvian embroideries circa 800 B.C. sport brilliant blue threads, as does the linen that was found in the caves where the Dead Sea Scrolls were stored in jars somewhere between the first century B.C. and the first century A.D. By the Middle Ages blue dyes had become more hardy, reliable, and available, thanks to the introduction of indigo, a deep blue pigment made from plants in the genus *Indigofera*.

Before that, blue dyes were derived from the leaves of woad, an herb in the mustard family. India was an ancient center of indigo production, and high-quality dye was produced there in great quantities. The color was made by putting the indigo plants, roots and all, in tubs of water with a mixture of fruits, wood ash, and other organic products and leaving them to ferment. Variations of blue were obtained by mixing indigo with white substances, such as white marble ground to a fine powder. Other shades of blue came from lapis lazuli, a semiprecious stone that was difficult to mine but had a deep azure color. It became a primary source for ultramarine blue but was so expensive that it was reserved for special uses. Because artists had to charge for it, it became a status symbol for wealthy art patrons.

Unlike blue, white in pigment or dye form is achromatic, that is, "without color," yet a range of recipes was used to make white pigments in many cultures. Lead was often ground into white pigments, which were used in cosmetics to make the face pale and wan, as well as on walls or in artworks. Other substances ground to make white included oyster shells, eggshells, and calcified bones from animals and humans.

The popularity of blue and white in a profusion of tones shows no signs of waning as we enter the twenty-first century. There are myriad ways to incorporate the color scheme in interiors, as the pictures on the following pages illustrate. This book will inspire you to choose blue and white as a palette for your own home, showing you the surprisingly diverse array of hues available today, as well as many creative and decorative ways to use them.

Tiles used to decorate floors and walls have been made in a blue and white color scheme since ancient times. With numbers, they introduce the color scheme on the exterior of a residence and serve a functional purpose as well.

LIVING WITH

BLUE & WHITE

It is easy to imagine any room in the home decorated in blue and white. This palette is so inherently pleasing and so much a part of the natural world around us, it's no wonder people of many eras and in all parts of the world have chosen to live in blue and white interiors. In the eighteenth century, for example, the color scheme graced Colonial and Federal homes in the United States, Regency and Neoclassical homes in England and France, and provincial homes in all three countries, in large part thanks to the fascination at the time with blue and white Chinese export porcelain. And the trend never died but, instead, waxed and waned as the blue and white palette was adapted to the styles fashionable in the nineteenth and twentieth centuries. Today we use blue and white with equal abandon in spaces that embody every imaginable style, evoke a wide range of periods, or emulate a variety of ethnic looks. Who can't call to mind a living room with an exotic Mediterranean motif, a dining room with a spare Shaker aesthetic, or a kitchen with frothy French provincial styling, all executed entirely in blue and white?

In eighteenth-century England, as well as in America, the fashion for handpainted Chinese export porcelain fed a general passion for things cobalt blue and white. By 1784, Josiah Spode had perfected the process of transferring intricate scenic and floral engravings to earthenware, and masses of his lustrous and affordable pottery were created in England. While many patterns are still in production by Spode and other potteries, antique examples are still prized by collectors, and displays of either can be nicely used as the focus or anchor of a color scheme.

Blue and white may be the most frequently used color scheme of all time, and for a number of good reasons. First of all, virtually every blue hue is compatible with every cast of white, which makes the duo relatively foolproof as decorating formulas go. White is a color we perceive as clean and neutral, and therefore safe. What better hue to pair it with than blue, the color said to represent peace, harmony, truth, and intelligence? In fact, studies show that people often choose to use white in their homes for its neutral appearance rather than out of any great love for the color, while blue is cited by most Americans and western Europeans as their favorite color. So it not surprising that the two colors are frequently used together.

Another reason for the prevalence of blue and white color schemes is the abundant shades and tints of these hues available in everything from simple cans of paint to a huge variety of furnishings, textiles, and accessories. No matter the style of an interior, blue and white furnishings can be found to suit it. Additionally, the choice of shades can influence the ambience of a decor. For instance, although the differences between whites are relatively subtle, this color can be blindingly bright, slightly off-white, rich and creamy, or silvery and lustrous, depending on the pigments used to mix it, and so white environments can range from sterile to warm, from antique to modern. The effects possible with blue are even more diverse

OPPOSITE One advantage of a two-color palette is its inherent simplicity—a real plus when decorating a tiny space. The rubbed blue decorative painting on the walls of this sleeping alcove embraces the bed in an illusionary sky, while soft white lifts the sloping ceiling. A fresh floral pattern on the walls outside the alcove produces a totally different, garden-fresh ambience for the rest of the room's interior.

RIGHT A majestic trompe l'oeil painting that graces the hallway of the summer cottage Czar Nicholas I built on the Gulf of Finland is masterfully executed to mimic the gothic stonework above and adjacent to it. While such painting is beyond the reach of most of us (not to mention out of scale with our homes), the pale blue and white hues, balanced evenly with a quiet blue-gray, create a serene and luminous backdrop that could be emulated in any space.

because the contrast between blues is far more discernible. Pale, powdery tints can create an airy, ethereal, or cool mood, while deeper values can be soothing and serene. Brighter shades of blue can range from vivid and effulgent to acid and electric—appearing powerful, playful, or dramatic. Finally, as blues move toward black, they become more authoritative and can be used to lend a space the feeling of dignity, stateliness, or polish, just as a navy blue suit is never-fail dignified business attire.

Yet ironically, white in its brightest shades is anything but neutral, while strong or bright shades of blue can be more neutral than one might

For a subtle and sophisticated blue and white decor, try a combination of soft shades in similar values, as in this room, where they are applied to stylish, sumptuous furnishings. The effect is nearly monochromatic yet explicitly rich and glamorous, thanks to the subtle differences in textures and hues. The shade of white on the walls has an imperceptible touch of luminous silver, which is underscored by the smoky, slightly iridescent blue of the silk shantung curtains and pillows, while the textured ivory matelassé on the upholstery is echoed in the creamy white that clings to the curvy wood furnishings.

suspect. The human eye perceives white as a brilliant color, and if a particularly dazzling or lustrous shade of it is used in sizable expanses, it will jump out just as any other bright color does. It can be blinding or bathe furnishings around it with an unattractive glare. On the other hand, darker tones of blue absorb light rather than reflect it. Also, many blue hues can complement one another, making it easy to use several contrasting and diverse blues to create one harmonious color scheme.

A blue and white palette can easily be accented with other colors. Green is a natural choice—think of verdant hills meeting the azure horizon. Orange, the color opposite blue on the color wheel and therefore its complement, can add excitement to the color scheme. (In fact, if you place blue and orange next to each other, they may appear to vibrate.) Various shades of purple or blue-green, which are analogous with (close to) blue on the color wheel, can be used to set either a calm or a kinetic mood when paired with blue and white. Because red and yellow are primary—or pure—colors (as is blue), accents of each will have differing effects upon a blue and white color scheme, depending upon the relative values of the mix.

Regardless of specific hues, color can be used to modify architecture and design. For instance, you might find it desirable to emphasize or down-play the structural parameters of a given room. If so, depending upon how you place it on walls and furnishings, you can use color to widen or enclose the space, enhance or diminish certain architectural features, adjust the visual temperature, highlight or hide particular fixtures and trims, or compensate for specific design deficits. Because the contrast in a blue and white palette can range from whisperingly subtle to vibrantly crisp, this pairing offers ultimate versatility in addressing both architectural and decorative issues.

OPPOSITE In this provincial home in France, a medium delphinium blue frames and softens the effect of chalky white plaster walls. The underside of the overhead boards is washed in white, the rustic beams in blue. Fabrics in warm, sunny tones, touched with harmonizing blue accents, provide contrast. As sunlight and shadow play over this space, the hues vary yet remain anchored by the blue-tinged white wooden floor.

PAGE 23 Here brilliant white for stately woodwork and walls minimizes the details of the rather grand space and creates a crisp background against which strong Empire blue really pops. The boldly striped upholstery is graphic, as is the perfectly spaced arrangement of blue and white china that dots the shelves. The austere ambience is softened by an Oriental rug and needlepoint pillows that introduce powdery blue and green hues. This would be a lovely space for a daytime wedding reception or summer party.

decorating in blue & white

While almost everyone responds favorably to blue and white, variations in the palette are incredibly diverse and you will no doubt find some more appealing than others. Some hues may be especially pleasing to your eye, or the overall ambience created by different blue and white combinations may suit your taste. And some styles of architecture just feel right when dressed in particular palettes, while specific hues evoke styles typical of certain countries, such as Scandinavia, Greece, or Japan. Choose hues that will make you feel comfortable.

The variety of rooms on the following pages shows just how interesting and adaptable this color scheme can be and how it can be applied to every room in the home, regardless of the architectural or decorative style you prefer.

living areas

The rooms we use most often tend to be the most spacious areas in our homes and, ideally, should appeal to every member of the family who uses them. While it may be the adults who set the rules for decorating a formal living room, kids are ever-present in the family room, dining area, and kitchen and will have definite opinions about the colors and furnishings used in them. Ultimately, it's important to have a group consensus and to let everyone have a say regarding the decorative aspects of these spaces. And remember, it takes more of every resource—creativity, budget, time, and physical effort—to make larger rooms come together.

In a formal living or dining room, you might consider using very pale, luminous, and refined shades of blue paired with whites that are a step

A nautical look can be achieved without resorting to the crisp marine blue colors usually associated with maritime settings. Here the colors are adapted to softer blues, evoking the sky, and layered on a pure white foundation through the use of fabrics crafted into plump pillows and breezy curtains. Only a few accessories with a seaside motif are used in the room, yet they are sufficiently powerful to emphasize the theme within the space.

25

OPPOSITE Thanks to bright blue shutters and doors and the wonderful light bouncing off the nearby sea, the white walls and furnishings of this room reflect changing tones of pale blue and plaster white as the angle of the sunlight shifts through the day.

RIGHT Blue and white can be used to interpret a wide range of decorative styles, from rustic or spare to frothy or refined. The dark wood furnishings in this simple kitchen in rural Brittany, in France, get a lift from touches of clear blues and clean white introduced by a backsplash of classic tiles, the collection of pottery, fresh lace curtains typical of this region, the tableware, and tailored cushions.

away from pure. Deeper shades of blue that are stately and/or sumptuous are another option for formal spaces. If you choose the latter direction, balance the blues with an equally rich and complex shade of white and disperse the hues in a measured manner throughout the room.

In a less formal living area, one that is frequently used as a gathering place for family and friends, warmer or bolder blues can be attractive, again paired with whites that are not totally pure. The same holds true for great rooms that incorporate eating areas, which explains why collections of cobalt

blue and creamy white pottery or china are often used to set the tone for these spaces. If country style is your choice, you can lean toward grayed and denim blues matched with off-white or ecru, or you may prefer clean, crisp French country blue and white hues.

While many shades of blue can be used in a kitchen, it is one place where pure white can be very effective, especially if the space has cabinets with glass. In certain settings, paticularly those that are sleek and spare, the clear or white light bouncing off such surfaces can be advantageous because it adds visual interest to the space. But since bright white tends to be inhospitable and cold when used alone, consider pairing it with warm, mellow shades of blue—or crisp blues that will balance it.

Thanks to the crisp contrast of cobalt blue against white, it doesn't take much to establish a strong color scheme in a room using these hues. An all-white kitchen acquires the theme with strategically placed lampshades, linens, and china that use the two colors. The popularity of the combination means that a diversity of kitchen linens available in blues and whites can provide an ever-changing display on the rack of hooks.

the psychology of blue and white

Color, whether on walls, furnishings, or decorative accessories, is a powerful tool that has been proven to affect our physical, psychological, and emotional well-being—and thus impact the way we function in our homes. Blue and white are no exception to this phenomenon. For instance, some blues, with names such as sky, sea, starlight, moonshine, lagoon, smoke, dusk, or Nile, are soothing hues that calm nerves and induce sleep, while others, such as cerulean, hydrangea, indigo, Bahama, and marine, can be stimulating and dynamic. While the range of whites is far more subtle, this color, too, can make a space energetic or subdued. Pure white is actually bright and dynamic, but some whites have hazy undertones that make them cool and serene or a creamy cast that makes them warm and nurturing.

It helps to understand the psychological impact of each of these colors when you are trying to decide on which hues to use. Here are some general guidelines.

blue

From its association with a calm sky, blue can symbolize peace, composure, and tranquillity. Because the sky is high above us, the color can represent coolness, a concept that is associated with heights; because heaven is thought to exist beyond the sky, blue embodies divinity, spirituality, truth, goodness, faith, and harmony. Thanks to our daily viewing of the sky, blue also represents constancy and loyalty. And since large, life-sustaining bodies of water are deep and blue, the hue can also represent purity and depth.

Of course, the specific implications of blue are governed by the value of the color. For instance, very light pastel blues, such as chalk, haze, murmur, powder, whisper, and crystal, create a delicate, serene, ethereal ambience that can also be perceived as detached and cool. Blues in the middle range, which approximate the tones we see in the sky or sea, are perceived as dependable, faithful, and harmonious. These can range from sky and seafoam to azure and turquoise.

When medium shades of blue acquire a tinge of gray, as in denim, slate, and feldspar, they become earnest, straightforward, reliable, and sincere. As blue moves toward black, in such hues as cadet, navy, and marine—all taking their name from military colors—it becomes more serious and authoritative and carries the message of leadership, power, dignity, trustworthiness, and reserve. In its very deepest tones, such as midnight, blue has the weight of black without its somber quality.

Not all blues are calm, sedate, retiring, or classic. Strong, dazzling, brilliant, and radiant shades of blue appear to be electric, exciting, and energizing. They are active rather than calm and playful rather than serious or earnest.

white

The issue of whether white is actually a color is perhaps central to the qualities and properties it embodies and symbolizes. In pigment form white is achromatic, which means it is literally "without color." However, in terms of light, clear white is composed of, and dependent on, all the colors in the spectrum, which may be why it is viewed as a symbol of purity and perfection.

White is also the color of clouds and snow, both considered spotless, and innocent. The absolute silence of a white snowfall enhances the perception of white as a quiet hue. The term "white noise" refers to noise that is virtually imperceptible, and the idea of "whiting something out" is to create a blank slate. The innocence attributed to white has made it the color of babies and brides throughout the ages—although brides in the West didn't wear white until the nineteenth century, those in many other cultures wore the hue. The ancient Greeks saw white as a symbol of joy, and the Japanese have long considered it pure, innocent, and virginal.

White most likely acquired its reputation for cleanliness when it was appropriated by the

medical profession in the early twentieth century. At that time it was discovered that the dirt and grime that could easily be hidden by dark colors could spread infections. However, because white shows dirt so well, it appears fragile, delicate, and refined. White suits and dresses are impractical and fanciful but also cultivated and romantic. When white is brought into the home, especially on furnishings or carpets, these same qualities are invoked.

Pure white can be glaring, harsh, antiseptic, and cold, and wherever this brilliance is used for decorative purposes, it jumps forward. But as white acquires gray overtones, it recaptures its innocence and becomes ethereal. Nature coats the feathered, furry, and fuzzy creatures that we associate with purity and virtue in these shades of white—for example, doves, seagulls, rabbits, cats, goats, sheep, and horses. If white is imbued instead with beige, it becomes creamy, rich, nurturing, and warm, making it an ideal neutral both physically and psychologically for any room in the home.

private areas

Dens, libraries, and home offices straddle the line between public and private spaces in many of our homes, so it is important to consider how these rooms are used before deciding which variants of blue and white to use. Deeper shades of blue work well in a room used for reading, meditation, or contemplation, but they need to be balanced with warm

A fresh shade of powder blue, balanced with pure white, is ideal in an area devoted to reading, since dark or somber hues can lull one to sleep. Thanks to a subtle overtone of gray in the powder blue, this particular shade is also neutral enough to be used on shelving that will house a wide variety of objects.

Consider using blue and white to create a crisp focal point in an otherwise neutral decor. Creamy paint and an important ecru and rose rug provide a warm, cozy, old-fashioned backdrop to this bedroom. Against them the white quilt, jaunty blue and white bedskirt, and airy white-on-white curtains reach out and grab your attention.

whites so they don't feel somber. Brighter and lighter blues are more appropriate for a home office, because dark hues can encourage inaction. Of course, whether a room is primarily used by day or by night, with natural or artificial light, will also affect your ultimate choice.

Often seen as cool, tranquil, and soothing, blue has long been the color of choice for bedrooms. If you use your bedroom to unwind and relax, you may find that serene shades of blue with watery, hazy, or smoky overtones, coupled with ethereal shades of white, are the perfect option. But if your bedroom does double duty as a home office or entertainment or workout area, you may prefer crisper, livelier hues. These same concepts apply to the bathroom. If it is a favorite spot to regroup and refresh yourself, stick to serene blues and whites. Otherwise, warm or brighten the bathroom up a bit or it may seem cold.

The bathroom—along with the pantry, the laundry room, or even the inside of a closet—is the perfect space in which to indulge your color whims. You can be as classic or traditional as you like, but if you long to use a bold or electric blue and a pure, brilliant white, why not do so in one of these spaces, where it's easier to take chances?

Private spaces can also offer the opportunity to play on a theme—aquatic colors for a bathroom, clouds and sky (day or night) for a bedroom, true blue teddy bears or trucks for a little boy's room, pastel florals or baby animals for a young girl's room, something aqua for a retro pantry or dressing room. Kitchens offer this opportunity as well, but before you choose wallpaper, tile, and accessories all featuring bluebirds, give some thought to whether you might be setting a stage you will tire of over time.

A bedroom is the ideal place to go all out, take chances, and indulge a passion for Chinese blue and white. If you lean toward lively patterns but want to keep them under control, choose an assortment with varying ratios of blue to white. Here the wallpaper and sheets sport a prominent but widely spaced blue floral motif on a white ground, while the pattern on the duvet top and bedskirt is much denser—and thus appears darker.

STAGE

While a blue and white palette is uncomplicated as color schemes go, it's not quite a one-size-fits-all affair—and would be dull if it were. There are myriad incarnations of both colors, as well as hundreds of ways to combine them to achieve a desired goal in a space, be it a certain mood, a tricky or complex sense of balance, a change in proportions, or the creation of a particular decorative style. As you decide how you want your decor to look, you'll be adapting the rules of color for interiors to this limited palette and drawing upon your personal preferences, imagination, and ingenuity to create a singular and distinctive milieu that is tailored to the space and designed to embody your taste.

OPPOSITE To give an alcove off the larger living room a separate identity and make it seem larger, the walls are painted a lighter shade of blue, the ceiling and banquette are painted white, and the bay window is veiled in diaphanous curtains that draw the eye to the landscape. Because the color of the walls is a tint of the blue used in the sitting area, the fabrics move easily from one area to the other and the entire space is cohesive.

RIGHT When integrating a range of elements, such as paint, textiles, furnishings, and accessories, into a blue and white interior, you must consider how the colors work together throughout the entire space. A medium Copen blue anchors this country sitting room and works well with both the crisp white wicker and dark mahogany furnishings. However, the formal dark wood and casual wicker work don't necessarily jibe, so they are placed some distance from each other, with the wicker in the center of the room and the woods on the perimeter.

39

applying the basics

So how can you employ a variety of techniques to set the stage you desire with blue and white? When you are trying to decide how to integrate color into a room, it is critical to take every aspect of the space into consideration. This includes the way the room must function on a daily basis, who will use it, the quality of light it receives, all the elements it contains, and finally, how the existing surfaces and objects in the space relate to one another. As you plan, think through the broad strokes first; then when you integrate specific paint colors, wallpaper, fabrics, furnishings, and accessories, you will be able to evaluate the way the blues and whites work together, change the nature of the space, and affect the occupants.

function first

Regardless of which room you are tackling, consider the function of the space. When and how often you expect to use the room and what mood you want it to convey are both critical to contemplate before determining where and how you wish to use blue, white, and any accent colors. If you are decorating a multipurpose space, where the ambience appropriate for one activity may not suit another, use different shades in specific parts of the room, such as the wall adjacent to your desk or bed, to create focal points for the different activities.

Once you define the way a room will function, ask yourself questions—for instance, will the authoritative character of deep Prussian blue paired with ivory be pleasingly formal or too dramatic and constricting for your living room? Will a snappy nautical blue and eggshell white be fresh and energizing or too bright? Is white with lots of clear aqua too

If you are in doubt about how certain blue and white pairings will affect a space, stick to basics that can be easily shifted or fine-tuned until the results are satisfying. Just a few key pieces, such as a Chinese Imari bowl, a ceramic water jug, and a pillow employing the same cobalt blue and white hues, establish the scheme in this pristine space. Best of all, accessories that employ other shades of blue can be easily swapped to alter the mood of the setting.

When simplicity is the goal, try a setting that is mostly white and accent it with carefully integrated blue highlights that add character without overwhelming the pristine ambience. The cornflower and navy stripes are just bold enough to enliven all the white in the room. For this fisherman's cottage clinging to a cliff over the sea, the vivid shade of Mediterranean blue on the shutters and screened cupboard was chosen to match the water.

43

When simplicity is the goal, try a setting that is mostly white and accent it with carefully integrated blue highlights that add character without overwhelming the pristine ambience. The cornflower and navy stripes are just bold enough to enliven all the white in the room. For this fisherman's cottage clinging to a cliff over the sea, the vivid shade of Mediterranean blue on the shutters and screened cupboard was chosen to match the water.

high-maintenance for the traffic in a playroom? Is rich sapphire likely to fade in that sunny sitting area?

To get started with the selection of the blues and whites that are right for you employ a tried-and-true trick interior designers often recommend to their clients—clip pictures of rooms that really move you from home design magazines and paste them into a large, spiral-bound artist's sketch pad or notebook over a period of a few months. When you page through the book, a pattern of the colors that really strike a chord in your heart will emerge.

OPPOSITE The blue plaid of the table covering is a bold stroke within this setting of multicolor patterns. Set against the stark wood-work, the lively colors of the rug, upholstery, and flowers balance and give depth to the interior.

RIGHT Blue and white can form a pleasing "backdrop" to patterns in other colors. Here a floral garland on a light blue and white striped bolster is carried through the bedding, playing off the sunlight in a pretty bedroom.

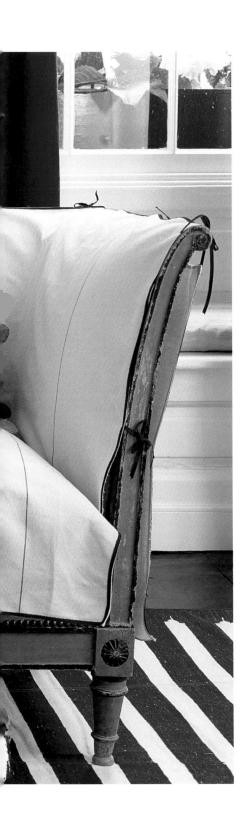

the balancing act

No matter which shades of blue and white you decide on, you must also determine how you want to mix them: Will the colors be used equally? Will one color dominate and another act as an accent? Will the overall effect be one of sharp contrast? Most blue and white schemes inherently contain contrast because there are no dark values of white, but if you mix pale blues with white, you can create an apparently monochromatic effect.

Once you've selected the overall hues of blue and white you want to work with, you can move on to selecting the appropriate materials—paint colors, tiles, wallpapers, fabrics, trims and accessories. This part of the process can be intricate and perplexing because deciding what colors or patterns to use for each component depends on what you employ on everything else. Given the wide range of colors and patterns available in blue and white alone, the process can be overwhelming—but it need not be if you work methodically.

How do you choose? Acquire samples, evaluate their appeal, and edit the possibilities to those you really love. You'll find an endless array of paint chips, swatch books, and color charts at showrooms and home design stores, but sometimes they can make matters worse by offering you too many options. If you find this to be the case, refer to your book of clippings and look at your wardrobe or any well-loved furnishings you already own; these will give you a pretty good idea of your inclinations and help you narrow the field.

To balance the power of blue and white pieces in a room, start with the largest blue and white elements. Here a lapis and white striped carpet, lapis curtains, and a cream slipcover on the sofa establish the color scheme, while a plaid pillow with scalloped edges softens the lines of the floor treatment. A tiny cushion in the center of the sofa throws the entire setting a bit off-balance, adding whimsy to the setting.

ABOVE In an all-white dining room, lively light blue and white gingham toppers and seat covers give an entire set of dining chairs a graphic, color-coordinated overhaul. Add to them a couple of blue and white bowls, and the room takes its spot in the ranks of spare blue and white decors.

OPPOSITE Indulge a taste for a bold shade of blue in small but intense strokes. Here the vivid French blue used for the window trim is reiterated in throw pillows. Cornflower tones mixed with white in the slipcover fabrics balance the ensemble.

design with a sample board

It is advisable to gather samples of everything you'll need—from the paints used on walls and ceilings to the textiles used underfoot, for window treatments, on upholstery—and assemble them on a sample board. Blues especially look different in various materials, are changed by their companion hues and a room's lighting, and diminish or intensify depending on the quantity used in a space. For these reasons a sample board should be as large as possible—you can use a piece of primed plywood or fiberboard (3 to 4 feet square is ideal)—to hold the largest available samples of paint colors, wallpapers, fabrics, flooring, and carpeting. Move all the samples around the room at various times of the day and night to see how the elements look under different lighting conditions (both natural and artificial) or from different angles and distances in the space. Also drape the fabric samples over the piece or pieces they will cover or hold them up to the windows they will curtain and again note how the colors and patterns look under different lighting conditions or from various distances. By using these tactics, you will better see how the blue and white materials you are considering work together, and you'll be able to make adjustments to achieve a harmonious effect. You'll find this to be an invaluable step for visualizing and fine-tuning your specific blue and white palette, thereby avoiding costly mistakes.

floors, walls, and ceilings

When planning your blue and white interior, first assess the size and shape of the room, from its square and cubic footage to the configuration of its ceilings and walls, because color and pattern on various surfaces have a huge impact on the way a space will feel. In practice, whatever shades you use on ceilings and walls will constitute about two-thirds of a room's color. Stronger blues and graphically dense blue-on-blue or blue and white patterns will make the room seem smaller and more intense, while pale solid blues and whites and open patterns, especially those with a light background, will make the room seem larger. Also, white or light blue ceilings

LEFT Although the stripes enlarge the space and provide panache, it's possible to have too much of a good thing. A simple wood bench with a white muslin cushion is a welcome contrast to the insistent background ticking; the pillows are covered in a companion stripe.

OPPOSITE Use stripes to raise a low ceiling and make an attic room seem more spacious. This sleeping nook is tucked so tightly under the eaves that a headboard could not be used. The mattress and box springs are set on a simple frame, yet the sky, navy, and cream ticking stripe lavished on the bed and walls expands the space to make it seem as if everything is standard in proportion. The tactic of upholstering the ceiling and walls emphasizes the angles and gives the space a tentlike setting.

or vertical blue and white stripes on a wall will make the room seem tall, while darker blue ceilings or horizontal wall treatments will make it seem smaller and more intimate.

When decorating with a blue and white palette, keep in mind that bright and powerful shades of either are difficult to use on ceilings, walls, and floors, especially if you do not have the professional training to address balance, proportion, and lighting. Traditional decorating theory puts the darkest tones underfoot to anchor a room, the lightest above on the ceiling, and midtones in between on walls and furnishings. It is easiest to opt for soft neutrals on ceilings and walls, such as alabaster, pearl, rain cloud, or eggshell or soft to midrange tints of blue—azure or Wedgwood, for instance. And don't feel compelled to limit yourself to just one color; consider painting adjacent walls alternately in azure and eggshell or in graduated tints of azure. If you'd like to incorporate a more intense blue, such as robin's egg, consider confining it to a single surface, such as the floor or one wall, or limiting it to carefully defined details throughout a room, such as moldings or doors, to keep the color from becoming overwhelming.

In this room the soft blue and white in the large wallpaper pattern and the graceful bed canopy set the overall palette—even though the daybed and carpet underfoot are golden-hued.

furnishings and accessories

Planning the use of blue and white on furniture and decorative accessories comes next, although these decisions are intimately related to the hues and patterns you choose for the room's surfaces.

Start with the element of the room that is its centerpiece—perhaps a plump sofa or upholstered chairs in a living area, a massive hearth in a family room, or the bed in a bedroom—and decide what colors you want to use on it. Do you like toiles or chintz in patterned or solid fabrics? Do you want to paint the hearth? You can plan to give it prominence later by hanging a large blue-toned painting above it or lining the mantel with a stunning collection of blue and white pottery. Think about window treatments. How important will they be? Do you want a filmy sheer with light filtering through or a flowery pattern for charm?

Indulge your taste for a faddish or bold shade of blue (or even luminescent or pearly white) in small but intense strokes. Make these gestures effective by keeping them infrequent but daring. For instance, your love for an electric or strong shade of blue can show up as a single slipcover, as huge pillows for a sofa or bed, or as decorative accessories such as vases, lamps, bed linens, or a tablecloth.

56

You can work a blue and white palette into a room without cloaking the walls in one or both colors. Here, where dark woodwork is a given, blue and white striped fabrics provide light, informal relief. The deep red tabletop and pillow tie in nicely with the wood without adding weight.

picking a finish

Surface coverings—paint, wallpaper, fabric, tile, laminates—come in a variety of finishes that affect the way their colors look in a room. Some finishes are totally flat or matte; some have a moderate amount of shine; and some are very shiny and reflective. With paint colors the choice of finish is usually yours to make (flat or matte for no shine; pearl, eggshell, satin, or semigloss for

some shine; and gloss or high gloss for reflective shine). For wallpaper you may have limited choices; and for ceramic tile, possibly no choice. For a stone surface—white marble or blue limestone or soapstone, for example—you may be able to select a matte or glossy polishing process. In some cases the finish is integral to the material, as it is for most types of fabric. For instance, you might find the same shade of blue in a chintz or moiré (fairly shiny), velvet or velveteen (subtle sheen), and canvas or calico (matte).

Of course, the finish of a material plays a role in its durability. In the case of fabric, be it formal or casual, if you are choosing a finish just for its decorative effect, consider the ways sheen affects color.

- A matte finish is more subtle, less assertive.

- Blue materials absorb more available light and heat, especially if they are dark.

- A glossier finish draws attention to its color. It will reflect more light, as well as any other hues that are near it.

When using a specific scheme like blue and white in a room or throughout a house, make sure you either mix colors of equal value and/or intensity for room-to-room flow or break the monotony of very light colors with stronger ones to maintain balance within each space. For instance, in a room that has an array of upholstered pieces covered in cornflower blues ranging from very pale to quite intense, make sure the different values are dispersed evenly throughout the room. Or consider using large pillows in deep sapphire blue to punctuate a subtle or delicate pale blue and alabaster scheme.

59

Use all white and fine blue and white stripes to dress a seat below a dark window frame—they'll capture the sunlight pouring through the glass or offer an uplifting respite on a rainy day.

PATTERNS IN

BLUE&WHITE

Pattern is arguably the easiest way to integrate a blue and white color scheme into a home. Whether flowery chintz, graphic stripes or checks, pattern can be applied to any element of a room, from the walls, ceilings, and floors that define the space to the furnishings and accessories that fill it. Best of all, pattern can imbue a space with a wide range of effects, calling to mind specific styles and particular periods or setting an overall mood. The effects of pattern are especially evocative when only blues and whites are used. For instance, cheery light blue and buttery white gingham checks can swathe a room in country style, while painted tiles in porcelain white and cobalt blue can create ethnically inspired effects. Dense geometric motifs transport you to Morocco, freewheeling, exuberant patterns conjure up Italy, Greece, or Mexico. Soft blues and creamy biscuit hues can call a Swedish aesthetic to mind; Oriental floral and landscape motifs in pure blue on porcelain white may mimic the blend of colonial eclecticism of the Victorians; and Napoleonic bees in rich Prussian blue and linen white can instill a space with Empire grandeur. As for mood, delicate powder blue flowers on a vellum background are indisputably

Turn a piece of furniture into the striking focal point of a room. Here a bold marine blue and deck white striped piqué, welted with sturdy cording and hemmed with ribbon tape in the same hue as the dark stripe, grants an ordinary settee a dignified yet stylish stature. Pillows covered in prominently contrasting shirtings break up the rigid verticals.

64

feminine and romantic; natty navy and bright white stripes create a nautical or crisp impression; and pictorial toiles in royal blue and cream evoke the romantic eighteenth-century air of French boudoirs completely upholstered in fabrics with sheep and shepherdesses. Additionally, motifs can be used to establish a theme or reiterate the purpose of a room—a print with blue baby animals will identify a nursery, while turquoise and aqua fish floating onmarine waves might be perfect for a bathroom.

LEFT Always give the eye a place to rest. Whisper-blue walls above the chair rail and a chaise upholstered in a subtle cream brocade offer a respite from the bold stripes on the dado and rug.

OPPOSITE A sofa is such a dominant piece of furniture that any pattern you use for it becomes a focus. Reduce the visual importance of a sofa by sticking to a simple pattern with little contrast to the walls, floor, and other furnishings. Here a narrow tailored stripe in navy and morning glory on ironstone white counterbalances the fanciful carved frame of the settee and gives it a fine, sophisticated vitality—the stripes even tone down the ruffled skirt. The walls and floor are left unadorned so they don't fight for attention.

positioning pattern

Where should you put pattern? How can you strike a balance between large-, medium-, and small-scale motifs? When do you need "solid relief"? Knowing how and where to use pattern requires an ability to match hues and balance designs. Here are some pragmatic tips to use as a guideline.

CONSIDER PLACEMENT: The eye needs a space to rest in every room unless you stick to one pattern, so don't plan to cover everything with patterns. If you use a lively blue bandanna print wallpaper, cover at least one upholstered piece in a solid blue or white denim or duck. Conversely, if you choose white chintz festooned with a scrolling Delft blue ribbon for the

window treatments and sofa, you might opt for plain powder blue walls, white trim, and Delft blue carpeting.

CONSIDER SIZE: In a large room, it's often best to paint the walls a solid shade of blue or white and then distribute patterns on the furnishings so they don't overwhelm. But for a dose of drama or glamour, don't be afraid to use big or bright patterns in a small space. A hallway, foyer, tiny guest room, or diminutive dining room is not a space where you typically spend a lot of time, so any of these can be good places to use a pattern you admire but may not want to see frequently. Some patterns, especially blue and white stripes, can be used to make a space seem larger, while allover patterns are likely to make it seem more intimate. But don't forget to fit a motif repeat to the surface it will cover. Wallpaper flourishing a large blue arabesque that doesn't fit between *your* windows is not a good choice, nor is a 30-inch damask fleur-de-lis going to look attractive on an easy chair with a 26-inch-high back—even if it is the perfect shade of Wedgwood.

CONSIDER ALL SURFACES: Pattern works well on floors, window treatments, walls, and upholstery, but don't limit it to these obvious spots. Ceilings can also be effectively patterned. For low ceilings, stick to light shades of blue and white to make them seem higher; for high ceilings, you can combine pattern, texture, and color in an embossed blue or white wallpaper, or use dark hues such as indigo or midnight blue to give the surface intimacy and warmth. The surface of painted woodwork, whether colonial paneling, doors, or cabinetry, can be broken up with a wash of white over blue, given a distressed or antiqued finish, or the details can be highlighted with stripes in the contrasting color. These surfaces can even be stenciled or painted with freehand decoration. Counters can be topped with blue and white painted tiles or with a checkerboard or other decorative arrangement of solid-color tiles—blue alternating with white, or with other blues.

66

OPPOSITE When selecting patterns for the elements in the room, remember that opposites attract. A trim striped cotton covering a chair is balanced by a carpet covered with a curvy paisley and accented with a tablecloth that introduces a third pattern into the setting. The floral on the cloth is spare enough to complement both of the primary patterns in the space.

BELOW The floor is an obvious place to use pattern. For a subtle touch, use stencils around the perimeter of the space or even over the whole floor.

LEFT Stick to medium-sized patterns in moderate or subtle hues in spaces where you need a low-key or restful atmosphere. In this bedroom delicate stripes in ivory and robin's egg blue cover a plump easy chair, while thicker stripes in slightly stronger hues—namely delphinium and chalk—on the canvas rug and sheer curtain give a fresh, gentle energy to the background.

OPPOSITE A mixture of striped, plaid, and plain white linens on the bed offers subtle contrasts while reiterating the varied blue and white palette chosen for this room. Note that the bedskirt has two layers: a bottom tier in the same delphinium and chalk as the canvas rug, and an overskirt in a gossamer white cotton that lets the stronger hues peek through. A trompe l'oeil basket of flowers painted on the rug adds a bit of whimsy to the setting.

CONSIDER BORDERS: Borders can be used to subtly integrate pattern into a room, to tone down or rev up other patterns, or to tie several motifs together. Depending on their width and color, borders can lend plain rugs, window treatments, or walls varying degrees of emphasis. Contain a boisterous pattern with a plain border. Make a plain or softly patterned expanse more noticeable and important with a border of a graphic pattern in high-contrast shades of blue and white. Try unifying a variety of patterns used in a room for a rug, curtains, or wallpaper by edging them all in the same color border.

70

LEFT Wallpaper borders add definition to architectural details or even trick you into thinking details exist where there are none.

OPPOSITE If you'd like to try a dark wall color but are worried that it might close in on you, opt for tone-on-tone vertical-stripe wallpaper. Here a deep periwinkle paper printed with thin, widely spaced navy stripes embraces an imposing and very dark mantel. A large mirror reflects a lighter wall across the room.

selecting patterns

OPPOSITE Check the size of a large motif before you assign it to a seat. Here a bold white bouquet sits— and fits—with great style on a side chair.

RIGHT Some patterns are more challenging to handle than others. A mural of hand-painted tiles unites beauty and utility, but must be carefully situated in a space where it can be displayed in its entirety.

PAGE 74 Use important blue and white patterns on the principal piece of furniture in a room when you want to call attention to it. The large stylized fleur-de-lis stripe on these linens ensures that the bed will be the most noticeable piece of furniture in this room. To keep the rest of the space in check, the walls are painted a plain cream, and a restrained "repeat" of pattern is employed only on select windows.

Given all this potential, it's easy to get excited about the impact pattern can have on the decor of a home. But because pattern is such a powerful tool, it's equally easy to become intimidated when it comes to picking the right design. There are literally thousands to choose from, and they can be incorporated in your decor through various materials; fabric, wallpaper, tile, paint, and carpet can all introduce pattern into a space. Also, both solid-color and patterned materials can be arranged in patterns—fabric can be sewn into a quilt, tiles can be laid in patterns on floors or walls, and decorative paint treatments can be given to furnishings and walls. Even if you know what basic motif or design you want, you will probably still have many choices to make for style, scale, and nuances of hue, especially if you'd like to mix several patterns and/or shades of blue and white.

73

Confused about how to proceed? Like every "language," pattern has its own rules. Here's what you need to know.

Since there is so much to choose from, this is the point when your notebook of magazine clippings can stand you in good stead. It may sound simplistic, but after you pull enough of your favorite images out of magazines, your strongest blue and white pattern preferences will be apparent, whether they are a particular graphic style, the proportion of blue to white in a pattern, the way pattern is scaled to a space, or the type of material used. For instance, you might find that you've clipped lots of Provençal interiors with bright blue and white checks, small blue and white foulards with pink and yellow tossed in their floral centers, and full-blown white blossoms arranged on blue stripes—and all the patterns are on printed textiles except for a tile checkerboard floor. Once you know what you like, you can shop for patterned materials and plan the specifics of your blue and white interior in a way that is as true to your vision as possible.

mixing and matching

When choosing patterns in blue and white, don't be lulled into a false sense of security because you're working with just two colors. Pairing patterns is not a task for the inexperienced or indecisive. However, if you're daunted, you can rely on the expertise of others—wallpaper, fabric, tile, and carpet manufacturers have created whole lines of complementary motifs, much as paint companies have developed color palettes. If you want to assemble your own mix, you can judge compatibility by looking at an arrangement of swatches on your sample board. While you consider the choices, keep the following basics in mind.

pattern know-how

Feeling adventurous about using pattern? Here are some options to consider.

- Use pattern as a calming agent. Some of the most subtle and sophisticated pairings feature several different patterns in a tone-on-tone palette. Pick blue on blue or white on white, and choose three different prints in the same scale on furnishings, windows, walls, or floors. For a bolder statement, use three different scales (small, medium, and large).

- Change the visual dimensions of a space with pattern. Add height by papering or painting the walls with multi-blue or blue and white stripes and/or applying a patterned border right below the ceiling to lift it even more (this works particularly well in hallways). Add depth to a space by using a wallpaper pattern that has dimension, such as a sapphire background covered with white lattice interwoven with white flowers.

- Introduce a temporary look through pattern. Dress a room up or down for a specific occasion or season, or just try out a new look. Try covering formal pieces upholstered in teal damask with aqua checked slipcovers (or vice versa), or give your velvet draperies a summer vacation by replacing them with layers of figured white netting. Dress up a plain white tablecloth with an embroidered blue-on-white Scandinavian runner, or cover an azure damask cloth with a white cutwork runner. Wrap the canvas cushions on white wicker chairs with lengths of tie-dyed indigo cloth.

- Unify a hodgepodge of pieces, such as mismatched dining or easy chairs, by covering them all with the same patterned fabric—perhaps navy blue and white ticking or awning stripes or a charming powder blue toile. Or if you use a variety of delphinium blue and plaster white patterns on the upholstered pieces in a room, give them a sense of unity by welting them all with the same contrasting color trim, perhaps in midnight blue.

- Let a pattern inspire you to be whimsical and creative. For example, if you use a wallpaper of trompe l'oeil blue and white vases in a foyer, install real vases—perhaps in solid blue filled with white flowers—on brackets on either side of the door. Or pick out an element in a patterned textile or wallpaper and emphasize it with accessories that also employ the motif. A white wallpaper patterned with sky blue bows might inspire you to trim slipcovers and pillows with real bows in the same hue.

Snow Fox 1426

Remembrance 1447

Summer,
sweet summer

D3

ABOVE One sure way to mix patterns successfully is to repeat the colors but use prints of different types in different scales. Here a geometric (the figured stripe), a small floral border, and an exuberant floral spray share sapphire and whitewash hues.

OPPOSITE Limitless trims, patterned fabrics, wallpapers, borders, and carpets are available in hues of blue and white. Picking which ones to use can be over-whelming, so pull together favored swatches of the patterns you like and consider them collectively to see how well they work together.

MOTIF: Choose one blue and white pattern as a departure point and work from there, selecting other patterns to complement it. Remember that pattern doesn't stop with wall treatments, carpets, and draperies; it extends to furnishings and accessories. A collection of blue and white Chinese export pottery massed in a cupboard can have the same effect as a boldly striped sofa or vividly checked curtains. Think which choice you'd like as a focal point.

ASSORTMENT: The best principle to remember is "opposites attract." Curves should be balanced with straighter lines. For example, pair lush florals with simple stripes, linear geometrics with curves, and panoramic pictorials with tiny checks or narrow stripes. Balance a large print with a small pattern, and vice versa. If you want to introduce a third pattern, go with a secondary motif and keep it mid-sized—such as a large floral with a medium geometric and a tiny stripe.

79

SCALE: Consider the scale of a pattern in relation to the size of the surface it will cover. You might think large prints belong on walls or long curtains, but a large motif well placed on an upholstered piece can be very striking. A small allover pattern that is distinctive on a boudoir pillow will have less impact on a duvet cover—but could still be a good choice because it might have just enough presence not to be boring. Always view a large swatch of a pattern you like from a distance before making any commitments, keeping in mind that patterns change as you move away from them. Small blue and white or blue-on-blue patterns can merge into a single hue or seem plain; too much of a busy pattern may make your eyes swim; and large expanses of large patterns can be overwhelming.

COLOR: Using a blue and white scheme can seem self-limiting because only two colors are involved, but blue and white actually offer a very diverse palette. It is always safe to mix different tints and shades of a single hue, such as a range of Copen blues with chalk whites, sea blues with ice-cap whites, or gray-blues with hazy whites, especially if more than two patterns are used in the same space. But this can be boring. One way you can diversify a mix is to pick a principal pattern that contains assorted blues, then pick some other patterns (and solids) that feature the same hues in different proportions. When you want to introduce a third or even fourth color to accent the mix, start with the complementary colors of the principal blue hue (get a color wheel and use it).

sources of pattern

When picking and choosing patterns in blue and white, don't think only of wallpaper and fabrics. Beautifully coordinated lines of wallpapers and textiles are one of the most popular offerings in home stores today and encompass every style of decor and type of motif. But don't forget to explore other sources that can be equally effective or satisfying.

Of these sources, paint is perhaps the most obvious. It can be applied in a huge range of decorative techniques, from sponging, stenciling, and stamping to mural painting and trompe l'oeil. For the most part, decorative paint techniques can transform walls, woodwork,

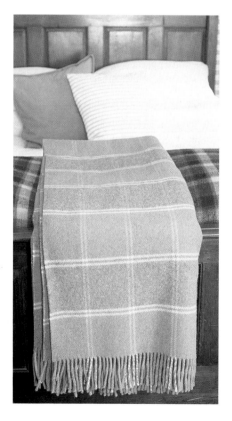

LEFT Using several shades of blue in the design requires a careful balancing act. Here a deep blue plaid blanket that combines many shades of blue is used as the jumping-off point for a blanket in a related shade of blue and a turquoise pillow.

OPPOSITE Evaluate the scale of a pattern used on the piece it is covering in relation to the other elements in the room. In a room that is predominantly white, a graphic denim blue ticking striped with white is used on a stocky chair and countered with a sofa that is covered in a similar striping, in reverse, white striped with denim blue.

ceilings, and floors into truly one-of-a-kind backgrounds, although there are wallpapers that simulate some of the same effects. Natural choices in blue and white include sky and cloud effects, starry night effects, and stenciling, especially in traditional American or Swedish motifs.

Carpets and tiles are other routine but sometimes neglected options for those who want to employ pattern. Both wall-to-wall carpeting and area rugs are viable choices that can imbue large spaces with pattern. Rugs offer a particularly diverse source of blue and white pattern styles, Chinese pile, flat-weave country plaids and stripes, whimsical hooked patterns, or Persian designs in rich, deep blues and aquamarines. Tiles also come in many incarnations, both patterned and plain. For instance, ceramic tiles that incorporate the same motifs as blue and white china are quite common,

ABOVE The blue floral urn in the slipcover mixes happily with the leafy stripe-skirted cushion.

OPPOSITE Here is a hushed and unified palette of motifs, fairly uniform in scale.

pick your pattern

Patterns range from a simple stripe or check to a sophisticated and intricate paisley or pictorial. Interpretations of almost any motif can range from staid and conservative to jaunty or outright riotous, depending on the style of rendering and the shades of blue and white. Patterns can be incised, painted, printed, or woven, depending on what is appropriate for the material. Texture also creates pattern. Here is a rundown of the broad categories to explore when choosing patterns for an interior.

Geometrics: Stripes, checks, plaids, circles, and triangles are all patterns that are widely available in diverse proportions and almost any imaginable hue. When these patterns are precise and relatively structured, they can impart a sense of order or they can be arranged to create bold or riotous effects or optical illusions. And they need not be precisely drafted; geometrics with a hand-drawn appearance give a contemporary effect.

Florals: Delicate little blooms in soft blue and cream are very different from florid blue hydrangeas or peonies emblazoned on a white ground. Blue and white florals run the gamut from sweet, subtle, and charming to big, brazen, and bold; they can be found in styles typical of many eras and regions.

Motifs: The repeating designs of motifs fall into two basic categories—invented shapes, such as paisleys, Greek keys, swirls, and trefoils, and figurative shapes inspired by nature or the world around us, such as shells, animals, flowers, and cherubs. Specific motifs tend to go in and out of fashion; you'll find them more or less available, in greater or more limited blue and white colors, as the taste of the times changes.

Combinations: Shapes, motifs, and designs can be combined to form complex, repeating patterns. The arabesque, a design of intertwined floral and geometric figures, is one such pattern. Others include intricate Provençal prints that blend flowers, paisleys, swirls, and leaves and patterns that incorporate repetitive shapes and contained areas of pictorials.

Textures: Although apparently "plain," many surfaces that are not smooth or opaque introduce subtle pattern as they interact with light. Rustic blue slate, handmade blue or white glazed tiles, pile carpets, beautifully hued blue raw silks of any weight, and gauzy or netted fabrics all fall into this category. Texture can also be patterned; tiles sculpted with relief motifs, lace, eyelet, cutwork, damask, and velvet burn-outs can be painted as monochromatic schemes of blue or all white.

Pictorials: Although it can be difficult to make a distinction between motifs and pictorials, the latter are compositions featuring several motifs or figures used in a repetitive manner on wallpaper or fabric. They are usually scenic, incorporating a whole structure, be it a cottage, a palace, or a scene from life or history with one or several characters. Toiles—textiles printed with pastoral or Oriental scenes in a single color on white or ecru, notably those produced in Jouy, France—are one of the most beloved examples of this type of pattern.

Used creatively, pattern can bring a space with tall proportions down to comfortable human scale. Introduce horizontal lines with a dado, border, and, as here, molding-framed wallpaper panels, using different sapphire and cream prints for each. If you hang a symmetrical arrangement of blue and white plates low in each panel, they'll help the eye to travel around rather than up.

as are the vibrant smalti and vitreous glass tiles used for mosaics. While the patterned versions can be used as is or even mixed and matched to create interesting and lively expanses on a variety of surfaces, plain tiles can be likewise employed and give you the same leeway as paint to create your own motifs. Even linoleum tiles in shades of blue and white are an option to explore, especially since they can easily be cut and laid down in geometric motifs by the do-it-yourselfer.

Decorative trim is an element that is often overlooked but is an ideal and effective source of pattern. It can be applied to virtually any kind of furnishings that use textiles, from window treatments and bed or table linens to lampshades and upholstery. Trims can even be used to embellish woodwork, such as banisters, railings, and the edges of shelves. Look for blue and white flat trims woven in stripes or jacquard patterns and all sorts of fringes, twisted cords, and tassels.

BLUE & WHITE

TABLESCAPES

The blue and white color scheme has a long tradition of turning up on tables, and for good reason. As a classic and popular color combination, blue and white has been used to embellish linens and ceramics of every style, from casual and warm to formal and refined. Since sharing the pleasures of the table with family and friends is what many of us do daily, why not make the settings as attractive as possible? A pretty table makes any meal more enjoyable. Anyone enamored with blue and white has plenty of choices for creating a personal setting for an inviting table.

First of all, you have a wealth of pieces to choose from, since every type of ceramic vessel, serving piece, or dish, from refined porcelain to rugged pottery, has been rendered in designs that employ blue and white. The tradition of pairing these two hues actually makes perfect sense because the kaolin, or pure clay, that is used to make bone china and porcelain is white to begin with and blue was perhaps the first dye color ever used. (Archaeologists have found true Chinese porcelain, decorated with blue, dating back to the first century.)

Blue and white china can be dressed up or down. In this setting an elegant lace tablecloth and gold-rimmed etched stemware combine with a magnificent collection of delftware to set a formal table. The multi-necked tulipière is a Dutch vase form developed to display the tulips so valued in seventeenth-century Holland.

Other tableware abounds in blue and white as well. Cobalt glassware, antique or new, might mix with rustic blue handblown glass made in Mexico. Whether elegant crystal or Venetian glass with blue twisted stems—the colorful pressed glass popular in the nineteenth century—period pieces are highly collectible, and reproductions are available from many museum shops. For those who have a retro bent—or for small children—plastic or enamel tableware is a good choice. Bistro-style flatware is available with bright blue or clean white handles. And blue bottles, both old and new, make terrific small vases.

Unless a collection of blue and white tableware is made entirely of museum-quality pieces, the best way to enjoy it is to use it. Here's how to create tablescapes using a blue and white theme.

92

RIGHT Blueberry blue and creamy white crackle-glazed dishes lend a sturdy boost of color to an informal table setting.

OPPOSITE Clear glass dishes imbued with blue add a fresh, watery demeanor to an otherwise pristine table setting.

OPPOSITE Strong shades
of lapis and cobalt blue and
creamy white linens brighten
up a plain white vase and
distressed table top.

RIGHT A variety of elements
can be coordinated with
dishes to set the palette of
a tablescape. If your china
features blue on white, try
reversing the balance on
linens or upholstered dining
chairs. The overall effect will
be more interesting even if
the hues are not varied.

getting started

Dress your table the way you dress yourself—and remember that nobody
wears the same thing every day. Try different approaches; they don't have to
be elaborate or take much time. If you already have a set of plain white dishes,
you can add patterned or solid blue accessory pieces—chargers, serving bowls,
glasses, vases, napkins, place mats, and tablecloths—to turn the grouping into
a blue and white ensemble. If you have these accessories and use them
frequently, setting a blue and white table will become an easy pleasure.

choosing blue and white china

Today blue and white china can be found in a variety of ceramics, in designs that take their cue from historic influences and in patterns that forge new ground with their innovative and imaginative motifs. Most of these pieces have one thing in common: they are a tempting blend of function and form. They inspire consumers to acquire or collect them and can be used for service or show.

ABOVE A plain white teacup and saucer rimmed with a subtle stripe of blue is neutral enough for any setting.

LEFT Collect an assortment of appealing teacups with a blue and white motif. Don't be concerned about mixing pieces in a variety of hues. Combine them with white china and clear glass pieces that are plain or fancy.

OPPOSITE Clear glass can take on a tone that echoes the color of the pieces surrounding it.

OVERLEAF The concept of power in numbers is reinforced by the drama of a mass of blue and white Chinese import pottery.

If you love blue and white china, don't worship it; use it. While you might reserve your collection of valuable transferware pieces for display, or use a set of formal gold-rimmed china decorated with Federal blue scrolls and eagles only on special occasions, you can have a wonderful time assembling everyday dishes and accessories that can be dressed up and down. Collect multifunctional pieces either with or without a decorative motif, such as flat salad plates or deep-rimmed soup plates. The soup plates can be used as pasta or dessert dishes, while the salad plates can be used to serve desserts, hors d'oeuvres, side dishes, or whole meals at buffets. And don't forget solid-color pieces; they give visual rhythm to an eclectic mixture. Or try mixing all-white and all-blue dishes (consider pieces having relief designs) for a setting that is at once spare and colorful.

In addition to classic Chinese export-style designs, there are eighteenth-century-style plates with scalloped edges and feathered blue bands, country pieces with checked borders and animal motifs, restaurant and bistro ware with contrasting rim bands, solid-color pieces such as Fiestaware, folkloric

An eclectic collection of plates and pitchers is displayed in unmatched but charming blue and white harmony.

pottery from Mexico, reproduction spatterware and spongeware, traditional Scandinavian designs and delftware, geometric Middle Eastern and North African pieces, oven-to-table baking dishes from France in wonderful blue hues and solid white—and the list goes on.

adding linens to the mix

Linens can help transform any table setting from plain to impressive when they're used with panache. Start a collection of blue and white napkins, place mats, and tablecloths to coordinate with your dishes. If you like to sew, remember that the simplest stitching can turn attractive fabrics into lovely table linens. Embroidery crewel or cross-stitch on plain linen can create very special cloths. Vintage linens are widely available at flea markets and usually are not so costly that you'd be afraid to use them.

103

Among blue and white options are brightly colored fabrics, such as vintage tablecloths from the fifties, bold Provençal patterns, Indian sari prints, bucolic toiles, woven plaids, and flowery prints. Ethnic textiles are often graphic—look for indigo cottons with geometric white patterns from Japan, exuberant batiks in indigo and azure on white or cream from Indonesia, and ikats from Southeast Asia. You may discover white cotton "linens" with blue folkloric patterns stitched in many areas of the world—South and Central America, eastern Europe, Scandinavia, and closer to home, Appalachia. Pure blue and white damask woven with a floral gingham check is a bistro classic—you can even find a vinyl clone for outdoor use. For a more formal dinner, nothing is more elegant than a plain white damask or cutwork tablecloth.

OPPOSITE A classic pattern such as Blue Fluted, which has been Royal Copenhagen's most popular service for more than 200 years, can be paired with a wide variety of linens to achieve different looks.

BELOW Traditional blue and white dish towels in an assortment of pretty blue and white plaids blend function and form when used as a tabletop accessory.

OPPOSITE A profusion of Blue Willow pieces used to serve tea looks glorious without table linens, thanks to the contrast between the blue and white china and the deeply gleaming table.

LEFT Delft earthenware takes on a different look when it is paired with a damask tablecloth in the same shade of blue. The white dishes pop off the dark cloth, bringing the painted blue pattern into focus.

Grape blue linens and glassware
on a white tabletop are an
unexpected complement to
the surrounding blue and white
upholstery. White china sporting
a pink moss rose pattern ties
in well with the purple tones of
the oversized hurricane lamps.
Is it coincidence that the
draperies sport a grape motif?

Blue and white place mats and napkins range from informal checks to the finest embroidered linens. For breakfast or lunch, consider using a simple place mat in a coordinating solid blue on top of a patterned blue and white cloth. Or use place mats alone on an attractive wood, glass, or tile table. Striped and checked dish towels make great place mats and napkins. And you're not limited to cloth—place mats come in dyed woven straws or wood, in laminated pictorial scenes and assorted other materials.

CHOOSING CENTERPIECES AND ACCESSORIES: Often the simplest enhancements are the most elegant and unforgettable. Grace a table with one dramatic blue and white cachepot or vase filled with white or blue flowers; arrange a collection of antique blue and white bowls or jars in the center of the table; or use deep blue glasses as accent. Tuck a placecard, with names penned in your best flourish, into small glasses of blue or white flowers in front of each plate for guests to take home. Ceramic or glass candlesticks are festive touches as well.

Gossamer textiles in cloud white and sky blue transform a white table and chairs into an ethereal dining spot that harmonizes with its setting. Translucent dishes complement the linens.

You need not start with
patterned china to set
a blue and white table.
If you add an informal
marine blue striped cloth
and assorted powdery
blue accessory pieces
to plain white china,
the effect will be casual,
inviting, and definitely
blue and white. Fresh
bouquets in the same
hues will make a
welcome centerpiece.

ceramics in blue and white

Ceramics—from china and porcelain to ironstone and earthenware—have for centuries been patterned with blue and white. Each ware has its own characteristics. For instance, pottery is opaque and relatively porous, while porcelain is translucent and dense. Thus pottery is softer, thicker, easier to stain, and heavier than porcelain, and porcelain is thinner, lighter, more durable, and costlier than pottery. The Blue Willow pattern, which has been popular ever since its creation more than two hundred years ago, has been used by many makers on their china.

types of ceramics

BONE CHINA: This form of pottery is similar to soft-paste porcelain (see "Porcelain," page 114) but also contains bone ash; it is thought to have been perfected by Josiah Spode in 1796.

CHINA: Although this usually refers to bone china, it was the name given in the eighteenth century to the many types of white porcelain that were made at the time, especially those pieces that were decorated in the Chinese manner in blue and white.

Delftware has always been painted with a variety of patterns and designs. A contemporary maker of English delftware, Isis Ceramics in Oxford, continues this tradition by producing pieces that depict a range of motifs. Some sport country motifs, such as roosters and other farm animals (shown in the basket), while others are decorated with elaborate formal scenes, such as a local estate (shown on the next spread).

CHINA BLUE AND WHITE PORCELAIN: This is one of the major types of porcelain produced in China since the fourteenth century, and it had a great influence on porcelain production in the West during the seventeeth and eighteenth centuries. The technique of underglaze painting in cobalt blue and copper red originated during the Tang Dynasty (618-907) and was perfected in the Ming dynasty (1368-1644). The process entailed painting designs on an unfired piece of porcelain, applying a thin layer of clear glaze, then firing the piece in a kiln at a high temperature. Because of the high temperatures required for firing porcelain, cobalt blue was one of the few pigments that could be used for decorating. Pieces from that period exist only in museums, but their influence remained until the eighteenth century.

CHINA TRADE AND CHINESE EXPORT PORCELAIN: The Europeans did not figure out how to make porcelain until the eighteenth century, when the secret was unraveled in Meissen, Germany. Before that, English and Dutch traders brought back wares that were made in the Orient strictly for the European markets. The porcelain made for export was distinctly different from what was used in the Orient: it was not as fine in quality as the porcelain kept at home; the pieces had a grayish cast under the blue patterns; and the designs tended to incorporate European motifs.

DELFTWARE: This earthenware pottery has a heavy, porous texture and was first made in England and Holland during the seventeenth century. It is still made today, but the old wares are much thicker and heavier than the newer pieces.

EARTHENWARE: Unlike porcelain—which is made from kaolin and can be fired at very high temperatures—earthenware is made from a porous clay fired at much lower temperatures. Because it is porous, eartheware is more susceptible to stains than porcelain, and is usually covered with a glaze to seal its surface.

FAIENCE: This is the French term for majolica, which is tin-glazed earthenware (see "Majolica," below).

IRONSTONE: This pottery was first made in the late eighteenth century by Miles Mason, an English potter who also sold Chinese export ware and was unable to get replacements for broken dishes. Bending to customer complaints, he made transferware dishes that could be used with export ware but were sturdier than porcelain. He concocted his own recipe, which included iron slag for strength, along with flint, Cornish stone, and clay. Ironstone is heavier, thicker, and more opaque than porcelain.

MAJOLICA: This term applies to any pottery glazed with an opaque tin enamel that conceals the color of the clay body. It includes delftware, faience, and the pottery called majolica made in England, Spain, Germany, France, Italy, and the United States. Motifs often are hand-painted or look so, and a popular style of majolica features relief ornamentation, often in vegetable motifs.

PORCELAIN: All porcelain is a relatively thin and translucent white ceramic used to make tableware, but each has its own individual properties (such as varying degrees of thickness and translucency) because each manufacturer has its own "recipe." Depending on its composition, porcelain is categorized as hard-paste or soft-paste; bone china is a fine form of pottery very similar to porcelain. In general, porcelain will chip in small, shell-like breaks, and compared to pottery, it is thinner, lighter, colder to the touch, and more durable, stain resistant, and expensive.

POTTERY: Unlike porcelain, pottery is opaque and thick, and it cracks in a line rather than in chips. In general, compared to porcelain, it is softer, heavier, easier to break, and less expensive.

A beautiful set of bone china in blue and white is better put on display than stored behind closed doors. To underscore its delphinium blue trim and to place it center-stage as an important decorative component in the room, the corner cupboard was painted to match.

SALT-GLAZED STONEWARE: Salt thrown into the kiln while stoneware is being fired will vaporize, producing a bright, hard glaze with an orange-peel texture. This technique was developed in the late seventeenth century.

STONEWARE: Although this pottery is only partially fired, the process produces a refined, strong, nonporous body. Stoneware is often left unglazed.

TIN-GLAZED EARTHENWARE: See "Majolica," page 114.

types of patterns

CHINESE TEMPLE: This pattern, depicting a temple with a woman and child in the foreground, was originally made by Davenport. The Prince of Wales chose it as his pattern in 1806.

FISHERMAN: Known originally as the Pleasure Boat, this pattern depicts a fisherman just catching a fish. Variations also picture another fisherman onshore. The pattern was used in England at both Worcester and Caughley, as well as other factories.

FLOW BLUE: A style of decoration rather than a specific pattern, flow blue was made in England and the Netherlands during the nineteenth century and featured various transfer-printed motifs. The name comes from the deep cobalt blue coloring used to make the patterns. The dye actually flowed from the design to the plate, creating a smeared effect in a range of intensities and varying opacities, which explains why these wares were also called bleeding-blue china. Collectors today differ in their preferences; some like the heavily smeared, dark blue pieces, while others prefer the lighter blue, more legible designs. Almost all flow blue was printed on ironstone china, which did not stain, chip, or craze as easily as porcelain and was also cheaper.

ABOVE A pure white pitcher enhances the color scheme because of the way it is positioned on top of an embroidered blue and white doily and alongside a dish that also bears a blue and white theme.

OPPOSITE An artisan-made contemporary delftware pot filled with daisies has a casual, rustic demeanor. But filled with sleek white tulips or long-stemmed roses, it assumes a more formal and refined look. Use it either way to grace a table and set the mood you want.

ONION: Meissen, the famed German porcelain maker, originated this pattern, which is based on a Chinese design and pictures peaches and pomegranates. The pattern has barely changed since it was first made in 1732, although it was originally executed in a clear, medium blue on a light blue-gray plate. A version in darker cobalt blue on a pure white plate was introduced in 1820. Manufacturers in France, England, Italy, Japan, and the United States have copied the pattern extensively, and many still make it today.

REGIONAL AND FOLKLORIC PATTERNS: Regional potteries in many parts of the world decorate their wares with traditional local patterns in blue on white grounds, as well as in other colors. These designs can be found on vessels and also on tiles. Types that are not difficult to find come from Mexico, Italy, and Portugal. Japanese tea and saki sets are frequently decorated with blue and white patterns.

SPATTERWARE AND SPONGEWARE: Beginning in the eighteenth century in England, earthenware was spattered, stippled, or daubed with a paint-covered sponge using such colors as red, blue, yellow, brown, black, and green. The wares were originally designed for the Pennsylvania Dutch market in the United States and were popular with this group of German settlers; transfer designs, such as tulips, flowers, a schoolhouse, or a peacock, were featured in the center of the plates.

STAFFORDSHIRE: Though many think this term refers to a style of densely patterned, printed china (usually in blue and white), it is actually the name of the district in England where hundreds of pottery factories have made many types of wares since the mid-eighteenth century, including transfer pottery, flow blue china, and figurines. Most of the blue Staffordshire dishes were made in the first half of the nineteenth century in Staffordshire, using

Thanks to the self-limiting nature of a blue and white scheme, pottery of every style and origin can usually be mixed and matched successfully.

creative napkin rings

Add a touch of style to plain white or blue napkins with rings. Though endless versions are sold in stores, you might want to create your own. The simplest napkin rings are lengths of ribbon, trim, or cord tied around rolled or gathered napkins, but these can be embellished or personalized with a few quick tricks. Here are some ideas.

- Take two complementary trims, such a thick, heavy grosgrain ribbon in a rich, dark blue and a piece of eyelet or lace ribbon a bit narrower than the grosgrain, and cut them in equal lengths, angling the ends of the grosgrain ribbon. Lay the lacy ribbon on top and tie them in a pretty bow around a rolled napkin.

- Take a cord of any variety, such as a blue silk drapery rope for a formal table or a thick, nubby piece of rope for a rustic table, and wrap it around a napkin at least three or four times to make a statement. Finish with a simple knot or bow and insert dried or fresh flowers, berries, leaves, or even sprigs of herbs or spices (such as rosemary or a cinnamon stick) in the knot.

- With elastic cord and large, pretty beads, make bracelet-sized napkin rings that can be wrapped two or three times around gathered napkins.

- Dress up plain wooden store-bought napkin rings by painting them with oil paint pens in a pattern that mimics the motif on your dishes, or use them as the base for a miniature decoupage project.

- A mini-wreath of flowers or herbs, braided sprigs of lavender, or a length of ivy bring the garden to the table.

transfer pattern pictures that depicted actual events or cities on white china. The blue patterns were the earliest, with black, pink, green, brown, and combinations of colors following. Each English maker had its own distinct border design, while the center designs were used by all the factories.

TRANSFERWARE: Transfer printing replaced time-consuming hand-painting, revolutionizing the mass production of decorated ceramics. The term *transfer* refers to the application of a metallic oxide design to a ceramic body using a tissue print. The printing can be found under or over a glazed surface (see also "Flow Blue," page 117). Many motif styles were and still are transferred to ceramics; pastoral and historical scenes, allover lace and calico prints, and architectural landmarks are common in older collectible pieces. Although multicolored designs can be transfer-printed, we most often think of transferware as being one color—often blue, but also brown or pink—on a white background.

WILLOW: Perhaps no pattern has been copied as often as Willow, the pattern that pictures a bridge, three figures, birds, trees, and a Chinese landscape. There are several different legends connected with the pattern, including the old Chinese myth about doomed lovers who fled across a bridge to an island where they would die together. They were transformed into two doves that flew over a willow tree. Versions of the Willow pattern exist from Minton, Wedgwood, Spode, and other makers in England, Germany, Japan, and the United States. First introduced to England by Thomas Turner in 1780 at the Caughley Pottery Works, Willow was inspired by an almost identical Chinese design sans the figures on the bridge. Spode also lays claim to originating the pattern, but not until 1790, when Josiah Spode is said to have adapted

Use napkin rings with plain napkins for a personal touch. You can easily make your own with ribbons and trims. To make something similar to this tea-themed duo, laminate printed fabric to card stock with a fusible bonding agent, cut out with a craft knife, and glue to ribbon ties.

the design from a Chinese landscape plate and added the three figures on the bridge to give the scene human interest. Original early Blue Willow pieces were hand painted, while transfer designs were used on later versions. Willow has been and is still being made by so many companies that it can be difficult to distinguish the old from the new.

makers

AMERICAN PORCELAIN: Attempts to make porcelain in the United States started as early as 1770. One of the earliest companies to make an excellent product comparable to the European versions was the Philadelphia firm of Thomas Ellis Tucker, which was in operation from 1825 to 1838, although the company rarely marked their porcelains. Another company that made a beautiful glazed bone china—including pieces in blue and white—known as lotusware, was Knowles, Taylor and Knowles of East Liverpool, Ohio. Overall, American porcelains from this period are scarce and rarely found today.

These three plates attest to the longevity of the Blue Willow pattern. The type of hand-painted Chinese plate that inspired Josiah Spode's design is shown at lower right; a nineteenth-century Spode version of the pattern is shown on the stand; and a contemporary Spode plate bearing the pattern is shown at lower left.

Painting delftware is still a complex and highly skilled art that requires a seven-year apprenticeship in Dutch factories. The color looks black at first, and the artist must dilute it to create just the right shade of blue. Once it is fired and glazed, the paint assumes the vibrant shade we identify with delftware.

AMERICAN POTTERY: Many types of pottery dishes were made in America from 1850 on, and some of it was decorated in blue and white. Some well-known makers include the Dedham Pottery Company of Dedham, Massachusetts, and the Buffalo Pottery Company of Buffalo, New York.

DOULTON: Founded in 1815, Doulton has long been known for its salt-glazed stoneware jugs and mugs, and today the company still makes a wonderful version of the Blue Willow pattern called Real Old Willow. In 1973 the company merged with Allied English Potteries and today is known as Royal Doulton Tableware.

123

HAVILAND: In the 1840s, New Yorkers David and Daniel Haviland of New York City went to France to find porcelain decorated in the English manner for their American customers and instead started their own factory in 1842. Other Haviland relatives followed suit, and the name appeared on many lines made by several branches of the family. Some of their china was decorated in the United States, but all were popular, thanks to their quality, beauty, and economical cost.

LIMOGES: Many confuse this term, assuming it to be a maker. Rather, Limoges is a town in France where many makers were located, including the renowned company Haviland. Other companies from the town include Jean Pouyat, Martin & Nephew, Martial Redon & Co., William Geurin & Co., and the New York importers Hinriches & Co. and Lewis Straus & Sons.

MEISSEN: The name Meissen is frequently misused and confused with the name Dresden. Meissen is a town in Germany, and a porcelain factory by the same name is located there. However, at various times the borders of Germany have changed with war, so Meissen has also been part of Saxony and Prussia. The term refers to any type of ware, ranging from stoneware to porcelain, that was made at the factory from its inception in 1710 to the present, but the English refer to Meissen as Dresden because of the factory's proximity to that town, while the French call it Saxe. Meissen wares have been copied extensively by factories in France, Italy, and England.

ROYAL COPENHAGEN: The first European porcelain was produced in Dresden in 1709, and the Royal Copenhagen Porcelain Manufactory was founded in 1775 in Copenhagen under the patronage of Queen Juliane Marie. The first dinner service pattern they produced was Blue Fluted, a stylized floral motif in blue on white inspired by the Chinese. (See page 102.) The pattern has been the company's most popular pattern for more than 200 years, and continues to be painted by hand. Another popular pattern, also blue on white, is Blue Flower, which is European in origin and first produced in 1779.

SPODE: When Josiah Spode was six (in 1760), his father died and was buried in a pauper's grave, and Spode was apprenticed to local potters. He grew up to found his own factory, formulate the recipe for bone china that is still in use today, and perfect underglaze transfer printing on earthenware to give us the pieces that are generically called Staffordshire today. (See page 14.)

124

WEDGWOOD: Josiah Wedgwood came from a family of potters but was forced to start his own firm in 1759 because his brother did not want him in the family business. He was known for his innovations in the field and built his business into one of the most famous and important makers of his time—a reputation the firm still enjoys today. Wedgwood made, and still makes, many kinds of pottery, and one of its most renowned products is jasperware, which features a blue, black, pink, or green matte base with raised decorations in white.

WORCESTER: The porcelains made at the original Worcester factory, which was founded in 1751, are considered to be the most popular of the British porcelains today. At the time the company was founded, it was named simply Worcester. After the death of its founder, Dr. Wall, it passed through several owners' hands, and in 1862, the new owner, named R.W. Binns, reorganized it as the Worcester Royal Porcelain Company. He was a great admirer of Oriental wares and had a huge personal collection of his own, which was used to influence and guide his designers. In 1974 the company acquired Spode, which it still owns and operates today.

125

ACCESSORIES IN

BLUE & WHITE

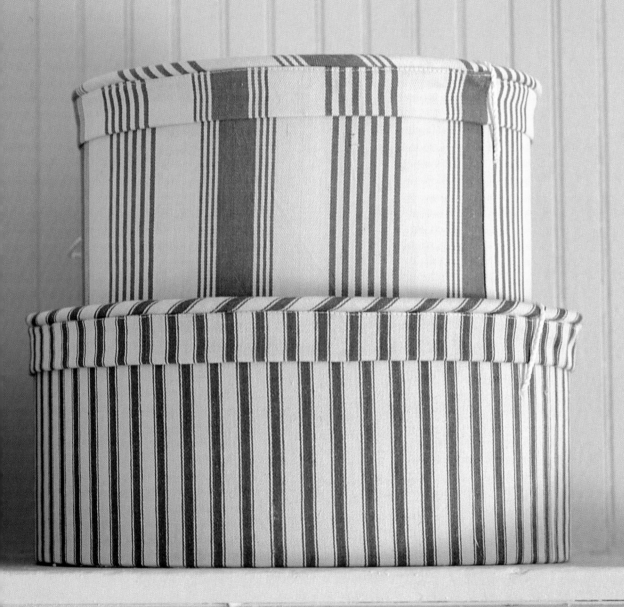

VOYAGES

Innovative, creative, and individual—accessories are what bring a blue and white room to life, make it engaging, and complete its ambience. When planning accessories for a blue and white room, you have a unique challenge. Your palette is established and limited, which means more of the same could easily be lost—and yet you want the finishing touches to do just what the term implies: finish the blue and white scheme and be striking enough to touch you with comfort, wit, or beauty.

Ask yourself how visually important you'd like your accessories to be; things that match the background disappear, but how much contrast do you want? Is this the time to add aqua accents to a dusty blue and cream palette? Do you want to enliven an expanse of white with graphic blue and white fabrics? Or break up a busy printed blue hydrangea wallpaper with delicate botanical prints matted in white linen, perhaps with a blue line ruled around each opening? If you will be massing objects in one area—throw pillows on a sofa or bed, pottery on a Welsh dresser—how uniform should the individual pieces be? All blue but in diverse hues or busily patterned? All the same pattern or assorted?

129

When the largest elements in a room are simple and unpatterned, you can add almost any accessories as long as the blues are pleasing together and the style is appropriate. Here vivid blue watering cans make a splash against a pure white sofa and distressed robin's egg chest; toile and striped pillows add a bit of pattern.

Are there unique items that you'd like to highlight, such as an old white teddy bear with a gorgeous blue bow or an extraordinary piece of iridescent blue art glass? Or is your room very spare at this point—even all white, because you plan to rely on accessories to bring blue into the mix?

exploring the elements

Since blue and white is and always has been a beloved combination, many decorative elements exist to help you incorporate finishing touches and frills. These elements fall into two basic categories: first, the materials that enable us (or someone we hire) to fabricate accessories, such as fabrics, wallpapers, trims, and paint, and second, the personal, singular, or even quirky objects that we accumulate and display in our homes, such as lamps, artwork, antiques, and collectibles.

RIGHT A blue glass platter with matching goblets serves as an amusing counterpoint for a painting of a covered glass food stand. A variety of blues is mixed in this tableau, drawn together and balanced by the large chunks of white in the space provided by the tabletop and chubby pitcher.

OPPOSITE Don't be afraid to use items in a variety of shapes, textures, sizes, and hues, but if there already is a lot going on, don't let the accessories get too busy. Here blue and white prints adorn a wallpaper border, upholstered headboard, lace-trimmed bed canopy, and chair seat, and so white-on-white embroidered linens were chosen to rest the eye. A blue needlepoint pillow and a soft blue bow provide balance.

fabric and wallpaper

This is the time to consider whether you want to pull some contrasting pattern or color into a space that is already dressed in unified tones and well-modulated motifs. If it is, reach for fabric printed or plain—in a special or singular version of blue and white, such as a lavish cobalt blue and old

ivory toile de Jouy or a turquoise dupioni silk that shimmers—and find a way to add them to your mix—be it in pillows, throws, a wall hanging, or a table runner. Or decide to add a folding screen or stack of boxes covered in a wonderful wallpaper, perhaps a sapphire blue and icy white paper with a Scandinavian-style print of large stylized daisies. When these materials sport exuberant, daringly abstract, or totally unique patterns, or are executed in particularly vivid or bold tones of blue or white, they are powerful and should be carefully employed.

You can also work with fabrics and wallpapers that are the same as or coordinate with those already in your decor, using them to tie together various elements. For instance, if you've used a cornflower plaid for the curtains, and you've collected a group of textiles in assorted cornflower and cream prints for a group of pillows to lavish on cream upholstered pieces, add the plaid to the mix. Unify the pillows by trimming them with the same braid or fringe that trims the upholstery. If this collection seems too busy, consider using solid fabrics in graduated shades from pale to deep blue on the pillows and trim them with piping made from the plaid of the curtains for piping. As still another example, let's say you've used a trompe l'oeil wallpaper border of cobalt and white teapots in your kitchen. Repeat the motif by wrapping the paper around canisters or storage bins or pasting it onto a small set of hanging shelves you've painted to match the cobalt tile backsplash. Or make chair pads or place mats in a cobalt teacup print fabric designed as a companion to the wallpaper.

trim

Just as a navy or royal print scarf can add color and verve to a plain white shirt or dress, trims can enhance a wide range of furnishings and complete a blue and white color scheme. A plain antique white or blue pillow can become an opulent confection edged in braids or

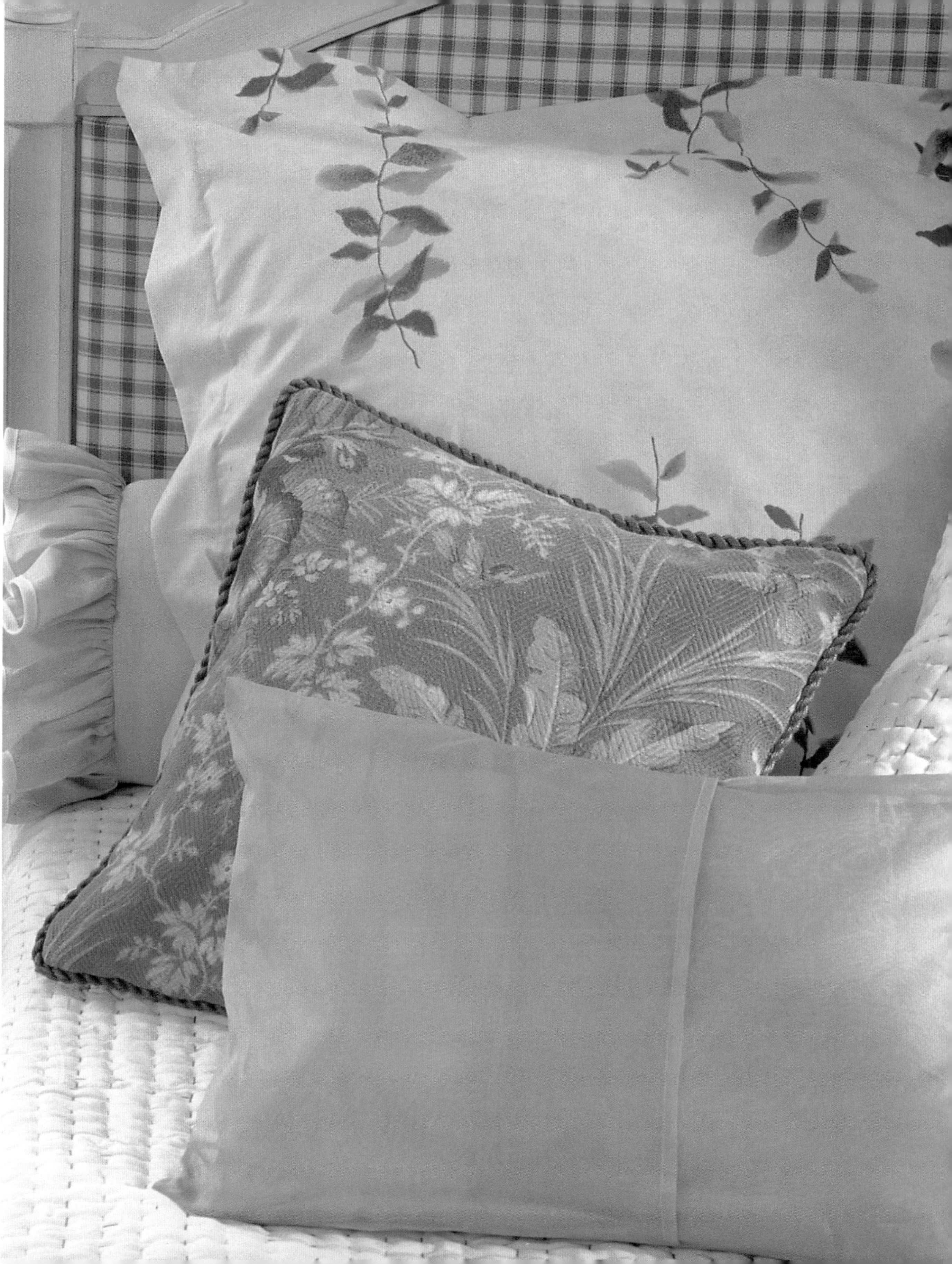

PREVIOUS SPREAD For charm, tie printed seat covers on a set of formal dining chairs. This blue-on-blue rose pattern is reminiscent of Victorian transferware.

OPPOSITE When you pile on the pillows, make sure you balance color and scale. The creamy white and ultramarine blue of the headboard and large pillow is punctuated by the smaller pillows, whose golden hues provide a pretty contrast. Blue accents in the fabric of the gold square and the blue braid around the edge keep the ensemble tied together.

RIGHT A flouncy blue and white lampshade with a pattern like those found on Chinese import pottery is interesting for its shape alone. A thin border of blue trim defines the exotic shape of the lampshade, causing it to stand out against the white curtain in the background.

looped fringe; twilight blue draperies can go from simple to sumptuous when pulled back gracefully with a silvery blue and starry white tassel-trimmed cord; and a host of upholstered pieces in different patterns or even plain shades of blue and white can become a unified and dignified whole when embellished with the same embassy blue trim. Trims—from smart grosgrain ribbon and sweet eyelet edging to elaborate tassel fringe and elegant netted lace—can be found in all white, all blue, and countless hues and combinations of the two colors. Your choice not only adds color, but it can determine whether the look is casual, formal, traditional, or personal and unique.

OPPOSITE Let lampshades lend a witty finish to the decor of a bedroom or dressing room. Cover them with gingham or shirting prints, then add ribbons, gimp braid, and button accents.

RIGHT Trim can add shape, definition, and weight to fabric. Red and white twisted cord piping provides a little contrast as it rings this white-on-blue linen chair pad.

LEFT An embroidered pattern worked in blue gives character to plain white pillow cases and adds a certain panache.

OPPOSITE When solid blue or solid white pillows seem too tailored or even dull, look for pieces embellished with bands of ribbon in contrasting blues—or add ribbons to plain pillows yourself. Here are some ideas: embroidered ribbon handstitched onto a plain powder blue and white striped roll is finished with bows for wrapped "closure"; plaid organdy ribbon criss-crosses through large grommets on an indigo pillow; subtly striped blue ribbon snaps a tidy grid over a large white square.

paint

Your options for finishing touches painted in blue and
white are limited only by your artistic ability and
imagination. By means of stenciling, stamping,
sponging, faux finishing, or distressing techniques,
you can use paint to turn fabrics, furniture, and
accessories made of metal, glass, ceramics, or wood into
customized one-of-a-kind creations. Painted
elements such as stenciled or striped borders can enhance walls, floors, and ceilings. In a blue and white
room, you can apply striped or checkerboard borders,
graceful looping ribbon and bow accents, morning glory
vines, baby animals, puffy clouds, American quilt
patterns and other motifs to any number of objects.
Finishes, such as pickling and transparent color wash or
marbleizing and other opaque effects, can be added to
wood accessories, such as boxes and shelves, as well as to larger pieces of
furniture. Your choice really depends on the style of your decor.

integrating objects

Decorative accessories, antiques, and collectibles reflect personal taste,
passions, interests, and experience and for that reason these objects go a
long way toward making a space original and exciting. Certain objects—especially lamps and hardware—are functional as well as decorative. Others
simply provide embellishment. When a collection is involved, the
embellishment assumes extra importance. Completing a blue and white
color scheme with decorative objects can be as simple as hanging one

stunning blue and white quilt on an expansive white wall or as intricate as arranging a hundred blue and white Imari pots on open shelves.

lamps

When looking for lamps, consider ceramic blue or white ginger jar styles in brilliant solid or crackle-glaze finishes or in painted and patterned styles, including new or old stoneware jugs with blue motifs. Check crafts shows and specialty home stores for blue and white lamps made by contemporary ceramists. Wicker and enamel lamp bases can sometimes be found in white, less often in blue, and these can work well in a French country, Victorian, or romantic setting. Lampshades can be custom-made in the blue and white fabric or wallpaper used elsewhere in your decor.

hardware

Don't overlook blue and white hardware options. Drawer pulls, towel bars, and other bathroom and kitchen fittings fall into this category. Ceramic pieces are abundant, and enameled cast iron is always another option.

BELOW Small, unexpected touches, such as these engaging drawer pulls, can add personality and character to a plain piece of furniture. Keep them all the same or mix and match from a variety of similar patterns.

OPPOSITE Glass lamps are delicate on a makeshift summer cottage dressing table; their blue and white striped shades bring a crisp focus to the all-white setting—guiding the eye right to the mirror.

textiles and trims

To quickly infuse your home with personality, mix blue and white napkins, tea towels, and tablecloths with a plethora of wonderful trims.

- Gather an assortment of pretty blue and white vintage tea towels—often embellished with appliqués, embroidery, and trims—and piece them together to make curtains.

- For an instant valance, toss a blue and white damask tablecloth—or several dish towels—over a curtain rod in an artfully casual manner. Use floral or pastoral patterns in a sitting room, animal and vegetable motifs in a kitchen. Or turn back one end of a white cutwork cloth to form a pocket and shir onto a rod for curtains that cast pretty shadows in a bedroom or bath.

- A pair of pretty blue and white napkins can be sandwiched over a small pillow form. Just knot the corners.

- Wrap plain white or blue pillows like gift boxes, tying them with striped, checked, or dotted grosgrain ribbons or bands of white lace.

- Tie back plain or subtly patterned curtains with blue and white twisted cord; thread tassels onto the knots.

- Use a hot glue gun to affix a gimp braid or tassel fringe to small pieces of furniture, such as ottomans and stools. Choose a trim made of mixed blue threads, all white, or mixed blue and white, whichever complements the upholstery.

- Create your own passementerie flourishes—glue thin soutache in a decorative pattern to plain picture mats or lampshades. Use pale blue or navy on white, white on a periwinkle floral print, ecru on white—any combination that looks right to you.

- Add buttons, perhaps the least appreciated of embellishments—pearl buttons, vintage blue plastic shapes, calico buttons (old white china buttons with tiny blue patterns). Sew them onto pillows in an orderly grid or stylized floral pattern; use them to accent curtain hems or tabs; or just mount and frame them. If you sew, incorporate button closures on pillow shams, curtain tiebacks, and slipcovers.

objects and artwork

There are many decorative objects traditionally in blue and white, including crafts, ceramics, and glass from all over the world, American quilts and folk art, and ethnic textiles. It is not hard to find painted boxes, picture frames, art pottery, antique art glass, buttons, ceramic animals, toys, and more. Sometimes a motif or theme is associated with one or the other of these colors as well—white lace, blue nautical objects, white birds, and so on. If you are intrigued by one of these, you might assemble a collection or repeat the motif in such a way as to complete your blue and white decor. Alternatively, accessories offer the perfect way to introduce accent colors into your scheme. Look for pieces that repeat your blue hues in combination with other colors or for objects in another color altogether.

Don't try to match artwork for your walls to your color scheme, but consider landscapes and seascapes with lots of sky, still lifes with flowers or blue and white objects, and botanical prints—the colors of nature will blend beautifully. Framed blue and white needlework and textiles are other options.

147

OPPOSITE Blue and white Chinese import pottery is all it takes to produce a definitive color scheme to a mostly white backdrop.

BELOW Against a white wall, a tableau of cobalt blue cut-crystal glasses and a matching vase establishes the foundation for a color scheme.

assembling accessories

When it comes to accessorizing your home and adding the finishing touches, there are really only two rules: assemble objects you love, and display them to advantage. Ultimately, accessorizing is all about striking the right balance. But do approach the process with a plan or goal in mind. Here are some thoughts that can help you in this process.

LET A COLLECTION SET THE TONE: If you already have a large collection of blue and white objects before you begin to decorate, you are ahead of the game and you can plan everything else in the room around it rather than trying to accommodate it after the fact. Use a stunning collection of blue and white pottery, a mass of frothy blue and white needlepoint pillows, or even a few (or one favorite) blue and white tapestries or quilts as a starting point and add other accessories only as needed. If your collection requires shelving, have it crafted to suit, or purchase shelves in an appropriate style and scale.

WORK FROM LARGE TO SMALL: The largest or most important accessories you have, or the most noticeable flourishes you want to use, should be integrated into a room first.

WEIGH BALANCE AND PROPORTION: We often have a tendency to use too many objects or overdo the frills. When creating an arrangement of accessories, be careful not to overload a surface or space. Be critical about the vignettes you create, moving and removing items until you feel the mix is just right. The more the clutter, the fewer details the eye can observe, so a large collection may look like a mass, while objects displayed in small groups may be more distinctive. Whether you lean toward spareness or volume, start slowly. Sometimes you need to live with something and observe it for a while before you can decide whether or not it works.

ABOVE If you're hanging white items on a white wall, or blue on blue, use contrasting ribbon as a hanger.

OPPOSITE Stand back and make sure accessories separate from their background. A broad moiré ribbon creates a pretty swath of Wedgwood blue above this side table, but its real purpose is to impose a break between the large and small busy patterns of the wallpaper and transferware plate.

PROVIDE FOCUS: Objects dispersed haphazardly throughout a room can look messy and unimportant. Pull them together to give them the status of a collection. On bookshelves group blue and white objects, such as frames, boxes, or small figurines in pleasing combinations, rather than interspersing them throughout for a busy, dotted effect. Another problem happens when everything is similar in color: objects tend to disappear. Be sure to have enough contrast between accessories and their background—whether blue

One advantage of working with blue and white accessories is that if you have only a couple of pieces, you can maximize their impact by displaying them with all-white flowers or linens.

and white pillows on a blue and white sofa (the scale of the patterns should be different, or trim should outline the shapes), pictures on a wallpaper backdrop (mats or frames should provide definition), or white ceramics on a table in front of a white wall (a dark tabletop or lighting should throw the shapes into relief).

BE ADVENTUROUS: Let items that seem odd or offbeat take center stage. The eye-catching, quirky details that often have a story behind them are the elements that make a room great—for example, a collection of American folk art flags, a punch bowl full of blue glass balls, stacks of indigo and white textiles piled in an open armoire, or yards of an azure trim that you picked up at a foreign flea market. These are the things that everyone notices, details that add excitement and warmth to a room.

Given a prominent position, a single unexpected or unusual blue and white accessory, such as this remarkable wash basin, can truly set the tone in a small room.

OPPOSITE Stylistically distinct blue and white objects can make a pleasing little vignette if the arrangement is well balanced. Here sunlight plays over formal and informal flasks and vases in assorted sizes to echo the deep and pale blue tones of the transferware plate.

RIGHT If you can, display vibrant blue glass where the light can enhance its translucent glory. A deep windowsill offers security and lets sunlight bring out subtle variations in tone; white walls set off the vivid hues.

BELOW Look for unusual accessories in blue and white. Here a large shell filled with small shells is paired with a starfish to reinforce a nautical theme.

OPPOSITE A variety of objects can be unified by color. Deep cobalt appears on the ambient votives, plate, goblet, and Imari vase. A purple goblet underscored by flowers in a similar shade adds interest to the setting.

SHAKE IT UP EVERY NOW AND THEN: Change things around periodically. Put a white slipcover on the cobalt sofa to bring a different perspective to those blue and white needlepoint pillows. Rotate the objects in a collection, perhaps placing a different piece on the mantel each season or each month. Restack the quilts in the armoire. When you make changes or move things to a different spot, you are forced to rethink what you are using and how effective or important it is. Plus, we get so used to seeing things when they always stay the same that we stop appreciating them. This may help you find a new way to use something or let you eliminate items that have lost their use or emotional value.

STOP ONLY WHEN YOU WANT TO: Since life is hardly a static affair—especially for those who collect blue and white objects—there may never be a time when accessorizing is done. Be open to change.

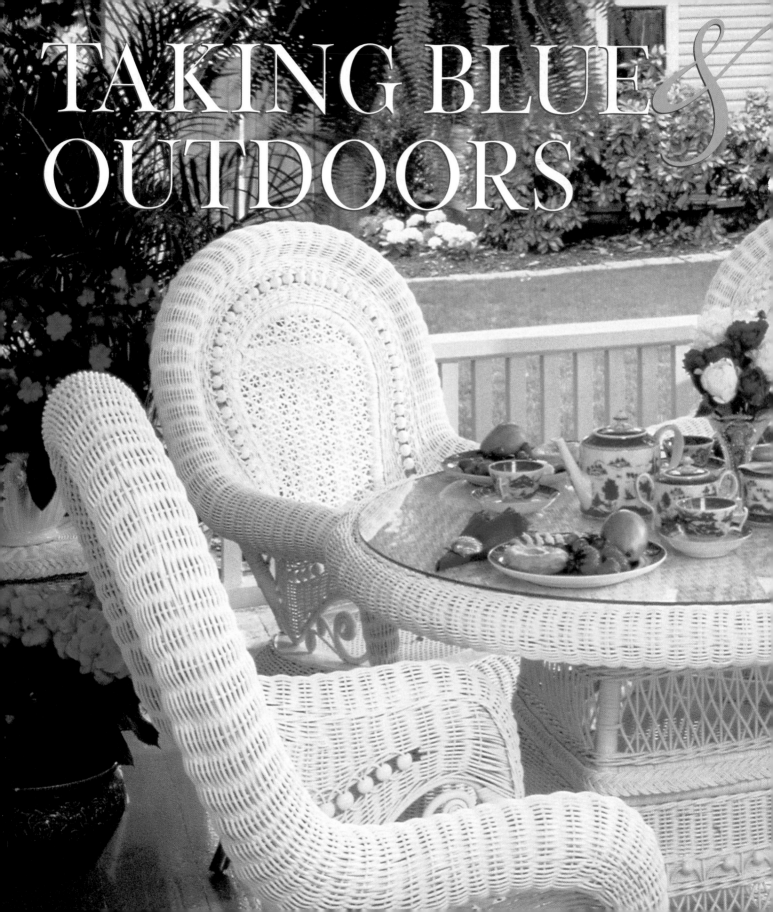

TAKING BLUE & OUTDOORS

BELOW Look for unusual accessories in blue and white. Here a large shell filled with small shells is paired with a starfish to reinforce a nautical theme.

OPPOSITE A variety of objects can be unified by color. Deep cobalt appears on the ambient votives, plate, goblet, and Imari vase. A purple goblet underscored by flowers in a similar shade adds interest to the setting.

SHAKE IT UP EVERY NOW AND THEN: Change things around periodically. Put a white slipcover on the cobalt sofa to bring a different perspective to those blue and white needlepoint pillows. Rotate the objects in a collection, perhaps placing a different piece on the mantel each season or each month. Restack the quilts in the armoire. When you make changes or move things to a different spot, you are forced to rethink what you are using and how effective or important it is. Plus, we get so used to seeing things when they always stay the same that we stop appreciating them. This may help you find a new way to use something or let you eliminate items that have lost their use or emotional value.

STOP ONLY WHEN YOU WANT TO: Since life is hardly a static affair—especially for those who collect blue and white objects—there may never be a time when accessorizing is done. Be open to change.

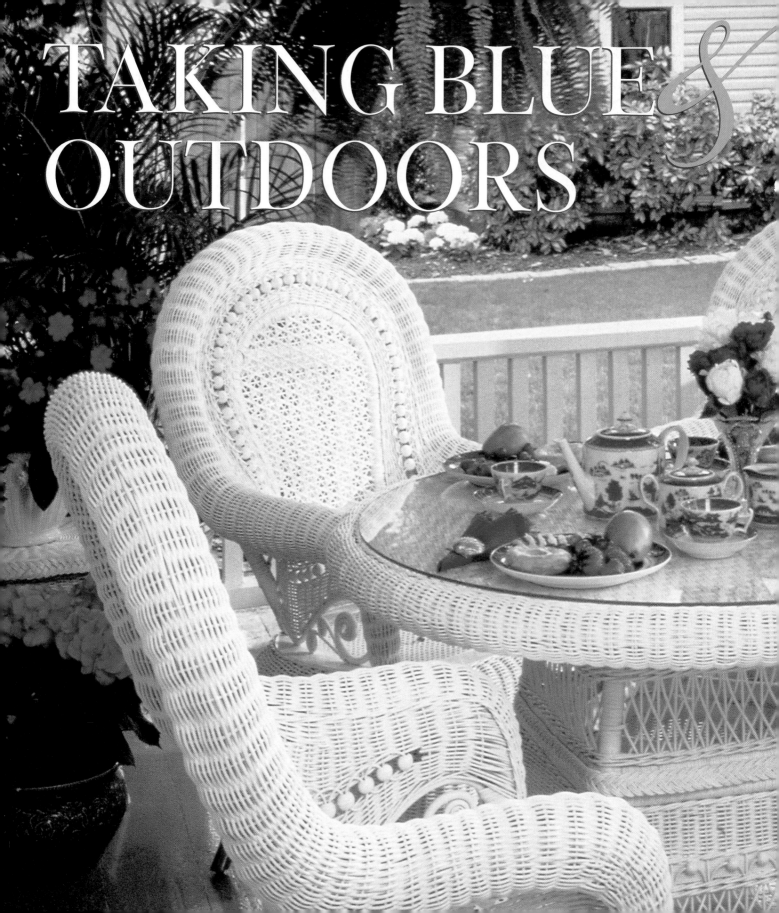

TAKING BLUE & OUTDOORS

WHITE

Ever fresh, blue and white have such a presence in the outdoor world that they are a natural choice for porch and garden decorating. Whether you have a large garden or a plain little patch of grass, a spacious patio or a modest balcony or deck, it will no doubt look inviting fitted out with blue and white chairs, linens, and accessories. There are two main differences between indoor and outdoor decorating—landscaping aside, there is less to do outside and there are more things you can't control. While the sky is often blue and you might have blue and white blooms from time to time, most of the givens in your outdoor living area are neither blue nor white, nor can you make them so. When you take blue and white outdoors, you want them to exist in harmony with other colors—assorted natural and painted wood, stone, brick, and concrete, myriad greens and browns, perhaps even a shimmering pond, pool, or stream. Add to this the changing palette of your garden: depending on your locale, your outdoor living space may assume different hues as the seasons pass. And sun and shade will influence any colors you use.

159

A shady bower will shield an outdoor dining room from harsh sunlight, and an abundance of greenery will show simple all-white and all-blue furnishings to advantage. Here natural wicker accessories complement sky blue chairs, blueberry china, and an antique white table.

choosing hues

To begin, analyze the space you are furnishing. Is it permanent? Is it adjacent to your house? Is it roofed or open to the sky? Is it a true garden room—an area defined by features in the landscape, such as an arbor, a hedged enclosure, or a terrace—or is it transient, emerging as you move furnishings about to take advantage of sun, shade, or a view? If you are furnishing a porch or sunroom, you can approach the task much as you would that of decorating an indoor room, with the exception that you must accommodate the colors of the architecture if you cannot or do not wish to change them. But if you are adding blue and white to a space that is open on all sides, your task is a bit different because the environment is likely to be changeable. With blue sky, green grass, and a garden full of flowers and foliage surrounding you in summer, let that season inspire your selection of blues for furnishing the space. Don't be afraid to take your cue from nature—color combinations that work for foliage and flowers will work on furnishings as well.

For instance, hybrids excepted, plants with silvery foliage often have grape, lavender, dusty blue, or silvery blue flowers—think lilacs, lavender, globe thistle. Plants with bright green or yellow-green leaves often have clear blue flowers—think forget-me-nots, iris, perennial geraniums. Get a nursery catalog and look at the photos to choose blues that will work with the foliage in your garden.

If you have an abundance of yellow or red flowers in your garden, you could use the blues that are analogous to yellow or red (that is, between each of

OPPOSITE Morning glory and butter white striped curtains set off this recessed exterior dining alcove, creating a gentle link between the weathered wood timbers, sandy pink stucco, and the rubbed white table and chairs.

BELOW If you are lucky, you may witness nature's love of blue and white close up. Is it possible a bluebird was aware that her nest of blue eggs would be so charming set in a viburnum bush abloom with white?

those colors and primary blue on the color wheel). In the case of yellow, they would be the blue-greens; in the case of red, they would be the lavenders and purples. Or if you want to create visual contrast and excitement, use blues that play to the complements of yellow or red, which would be the blues with a purple cast for yellows and the blues with a green cast for red. Or if you have a garden that is already color-coded with blue and white flowers, just pick up one or more of the blue hues.

On the other hand, because of their typically casual mood, outdoor rooms are a good place to become a bit playful, if not downright daring or bold, in a way that might feel uncomfortable inside your home. Consider using an electric blue and pairing it with a white tinted with its complement—lemon—and then using lemon as a third color in your scheme.

Think also of the amount of sun or shade, or both, that will pass over the blues you introduce with furnishings. Abundant sun will cast a green tinge over blue or wash it out; shade will add a purple tone or deepen the value.

ABOVE Painted blue and white planters filled with flowers in coordinating hues are charming accents in sunrooms or enclosed porches, patios, and decks, where they establish or reinforce the freshness of the outdoors.

RIGHT Flowers and plants soften the decor in this light-filled sun porch, extending the lush greenery of the outdoors seen through the windows. When the light becomes too intense, curtain tiebacks can be released to loosen the panels and offer some shade.

16

LEFT To create an alfresco
tea room with a blue and
white theme, move the
white furniture you use
inside outdoors. Mauve
blue and white china and
a turquoise cachepot are
an unexpected combination
that seems perfectly natural
out under the sun.

OPPOSITE If your deck is
a summer dining room,
use extra-plump cushions
to keep the hard wooden
chairs comfortable for
lingering guests. Here a
big check makes a fitting
covering, picking up the
tones of the blue lattice
on the far brick wall and
harmonizing with the
lush foliage.

setting the stage

Arraying an outdoor "room" with blue and white furnishings is usually easier than outfitting an interior because there are few if any walls to paint, floors to carpet, or windows to cover. And many such spaces are hardly permanent, since the accoutrements are moved according to the occasion or the season. If your outdoor space has no architectural framework, you can rely entirely on furnishings and accessories to create a blue and white environment.

painting the architecture

To set the blue and white stage for a permanent outdooor room such as a balcony, porch, or gazebo, decide first if you want to paint the architecture. You may need to keep it the same color as the exterior of your home. The next easiest option is to paint it white. White won't clash with the environs, and with its connotation of old-fashioned simplicity, it is a perennial favorite for porches. White will make any confining walls recede, and it has reflective properties that will bounce blue and any other hues about. Porch ceilings are often painted pale blue to give the illusion of sky overhead.

Those who are self-assured or adventurous might consider painting the ceiling or floor of a porch or balcony in blue or white or in two or more shades of blue. Or use blue and white stripes, checks, or polka dots. Clouds are fun on a ceiling; a watery pattern could be great on a floor. And don't forget one of color's main benefits, which is to work architectural magic. If you want a high-ceilinged porch to appear lower and cozier, paint the ceiling a dark blue; if you want it to seem large and airy, stick to white and pale blues.

OPPOSITE Tailored blue and white fabrics give a calm and crisp demeanor to porch furnishings. A simple extra-large blue and white plaid tablecloth and clean striped cushions look uncomplicated, cool, and inviting against white wicker and the hot green landscape beyond.

RIGHT A white stucco cottage is like a blank canvas, which comes alive when a contrasting color, such as this Oslo blue, is included in the picture.

furnishing outside in blue and white

Next consider seats, benches, and tables. Outdoor furniture made of plastic, resin, enameled metal, and painted wood and wicker is easy to find in white, and because cushions and coverings are so much a part of making it comfortable, you can easily give it a blue and white spin. If you are starting with pieces that are not white, chances are they are a natural wood color or green—two colors present outdoors anyway, and thus easy to work into your palette. And some outdoor furniture is blue (Parisian café tables and chairs, for instance), so start that way if you like. If you are setting up a covered porch, add a cupboard to store small gardening gear or tableware. Paint the cupboard blue and stencil it with white flowers, or paint it blue and decorate it with morning glories and bluebirds.

   If you enjoy putting your own stamp on things, why not give wood or wicker furnishings unity and charm by painting them the same shade of blue or in a simple blue and white pattern (such as stripes or checks). Or paint matching pieces or even a collection of old rocking chairs in graduated or assorted hues of blue, then arrange them in a row on your porch or across the crest of your lawn.

RIGHT A tossed floral print and stylized tattersall, both in sapphire blue and white, sit primly on this graceful white iron settee. Bring the cushions out for company, but store them away from the strong sunlight when they're not needed.

OPPOSITE TOP Porch furniture begs to be covered with summery fabrics. The hydrangea print and crisp stripe cushioning this soldier-blue settee offer a light-hearted invitation to lounge.

OPPOSITE BOTTOM Slipcovers not only add comfort and color, but can accentuate the best features of a piece. Here back and seat pads in two geometric patterns of blue and white emphasize the lovely lines of this rocker and invite you to sit in comfort.

Almost all furniture suitable for use outdoors lends itself to the addition of fabrics. Because of their nautical associations or simply because they always seem fresh, blue and white patterns are frequently found on any number of ready-made outdoor cushions, umbrellas, and picnic-style linens. Awning and regatta stripes, bistro checks, prints with anchors, sailboats, or fish, and fun florals are just a few patterns that are commonly available. Solid blue cushions with white piping (or the reverse) never fail to look snappy. Home design stores sometimes carry plain white slipcovers or cushion covers that can be painted or dyed in shades of blue and white or embellished with blue trim. For balmy evenings that turn cool, have an attractive stack of cotton blankets or shawls on hand (you can probably find them in blue and white checked or tattersal patterns), rolled up and arranged in bushel baskets.

Of course, you might want to use blue and white outdoors on a less permanent basis, perhaps just for occasional dining. You can set a blue and white table on your porch or in any suitable spot in your garden. Make it as fancy as you like—white cutwork linens and blue glassware look spectacular against green—or go for simple gear in bright blue, turquoise, and robin's egg tints. Whichever setting, add buckets, jars, or vases of blue and white flowers—roses, hydrangeas, delphiniums, iris, lilacs, pansies, and primroses, as the season permits.

Complete your outdoor room with garden-fresh accessories. Vases, pitchers, watering cans, flower buckets, cachepots, and baskets lend an appropriate ambience and all can be found in shades of blue, white, or blue and white. Choose from enameled pieces, glazed ceramics, and dyed or painted wicker; even oxidized copper with its turquoise patina. Ethnic, eccentric, and aged objects add romance to outdoor decor, and many come in interesting blues.

Don't forget lighting. Hang large Mediterranean blue or white enamel pendant lamps from a porch ceiling. Suspend blue or a combination of blue and white string lights from beams or trees, or use them to outline bushes or flower beds. Also place masses of blue or white candles or hurricane lamps on tables for both ambient light and an infusion of color.

170

Porch furnishings can be blue and white even if the house siding is another color—just pick a blue that holds its own against the wall. Here a bright French blue picks up the purple overtones of the dark wood siding. To keep the dark tones balanced, the strong blue hue covers the tables and the bulkier furnishings, while the chairs and china are white.

wicker furniture

With extravagant lattice patterns, lush weaves, fanciful curlicues, and picture-pretty white wicker furnishings have been fashionable both inside and outside the home since the Victorian era. Durable and lightweight, wicker is an ideal choice for anyone who wants to furnish an outdoor space, especially because the pieces can be as neutral as a blank white canvas as it waits to be splashed with blue and white cushions, pillows, throws, and quilts.

Wicker is actually a broad term for furniture woven from rattan, willow, reed, cane, raffia, fiber rush (twisted paper), sea grass, and other materials. It comes from the Scandinavian term *vika,* which means "to bend." A statue of an official sitting on a reed hassock dating to 2600 B.C. was found in Mesopotamia, and a reed wig box dating to 1400 B.C. was found in Egypt. The Romans and Greeks used wicker for baskets and furniture as well.

In the United States wicker became popular thanks to the entrepreneurship of Massachusetts grocer Cyrus Wakefield. In the 1840s he noticed that ships returning to Boston from China discarded the reeds they used to protect their cargo, and he recycled the material into furniture that was originally used indoors. He founded the Wakefield Rattan Company in South Reading, Massachusetts, which was later renamed Wakefield in his honor. The company eventually merged with Heywood Brothers to become Heywood-Wakefield. Although the firm stopped making wicker furniture in the 1930s, plenty of other furniture factories continued to produce it.

In the late nineteenth century, as people fled to the country in search of fresh air, homeowners moved their wicker outdoors to their porches. People believed that fresh air could blow germs away from the woven patterns, so wicker was considered a healthy furnishing. And if wicker were painted white, any germ-harboring dirt would be apparent and could be easily removed.

Through the decades, wicker furnishings have reflected changing design styles. Victorian wicker, in its heyday from 1880 to 1910, was fanciful, frothy, and often embellished with romantic motifs, such as peacocks and hearts. Other distinct styles also existed, such as Cape Cod, which wove fibers tightly together, and Bar Harbor, which featured open latticework. The Arts and Crafts wicker that followed was more rectilinear, while the Art Deco wicker that emerged in the 1920s was very stream-lined. Today reproductions are made in all of these traditional styles. Offerings in this intricately wrought material range from settees and chairs of every type to tables, buffets, and even bassinets and baby carriages.

accessorizing the landscape

Why limit your outdoor use of blue and white to furnishings? Perhaps
there are other ways to bring these colors into your landscape. Don't forget
umbrellas, awnings, hammocks, window boxes, fences, trellises, planters,
birdhouses, birdbaths, garden sheds, gazing globes, playhouses, or even tree
houses. Royal blue and white pennants or streamers could announce a
party. Closer to the ground, paths, patios, and terraces can be surfaced in
white shells, white pebbles, bluestone, slate, or a mixture of these. In the
right environment, glazed blue and white tiles can be used. Are you
planning a pool or small pond? Will it be lined or surrounded with blue?

LEFT A coat of dove blue
paint on wood lattice
creates a blue "wall" in front
of a brick facade. Open
French doors reveal white
curtains and bed linens.

OPPOSITE A big market
umbrella screens midday
diners from the bright sun.
This white canopy enhances
the clean picture presented
by romantic white linens
with crisp blue accents—all
shown to perfection against
summer foliage.

photography credits